Crochet Unraveled: First Stitches

A Comprehensive Guide for Beginners to Master the Art of Crocheting

Tammi Desantis

Summary

Chapter 1: Introduction to Crochet

If you're looking for a creative and rewarding hobby, then crochet could be just what you're looking for. Crochet is a type of needlework that involves using a hook to create a fabric from yarn or thread. Unlike knitting, which uses two needles, crochet uses just one hook. This means that crochet is an ideal craft for those who find knitting too fiddly or who prefer something more portable.

Crochet can be used to make a wide range of items, from clothing and accessories to homeware and gifts. In this chapter, we'll take a look at the basic techniques you need to get started with crochet, as well as some tips and tricks to make your crochet projects a success.

Getting Started with Crochet

Before you start crocheting, you'll need to gather a few supplies. These include a crochet hook, yarn or thread, and a pattern or instructions. Let's take a look at each of these in turn.

Crochet Hooks

Crochet hooks come in a range of sizes, from tiny hooks for fine thread to larger hooks for bulky yarn. The size of hook you use will depend on the type of project you're making, as well as the weight of yarn or thread you're using.

Crochet hooks are measured in millimeters (mm) and are labeled with a letter or number to help you identify the size. The larger the hook size, the bigger the loops you'll create, and the faster your project will grow.

Most crocheters start with a medium-sized hook, such as a 4mm or 5mm hook. These are versatile sizes that can be used for a range of projects, from scarves and hats to blankets and shawls.

Yarn and Thread

The type of yarn or thread you choose will also depend on the project you're making. Yarn comes in a range of weights, from super fine laceweight to bulky weight, and is made from materials such as wool, cotton, acrylic, and blends of different fibers.

When choosing yarn, consider the color, texture, and weight of the yarn, as well as the pattern you'll be using. Some patterns will specify the type of yarn to use, while others will give you more freedom to choose.

Thread is a much finer material than yarn and is typically used for delicate projects, such as doilies or lace. Thread comes in a range of weights, from size 3 to size 100, with the higher numbers being finer. When working with thread, you'll typically use a smaller hook than you would with yarn.

Patterns and Instructions

Once you have your crochet hook and yarn or thread, you'll need a pattern or instructions to follow. Patterns can be found in books, magazines, and online, and range from simple to complex.

When choosing a pattern, look for one that matches your skill level. If you're a beginner, start with a simple project, such as a scarf or dishcloth, before moving on to more challenging projects.

Most patterns come with written instructions and a chart or diagram to help you visualize the stitches. Some patterns also include video tutorials to help you learn the techniques.

Basic Crochet Stitches

Now that you have all your supplies, it's time to start crocheting. The first step is to learn the basic crochet stitches. These are the building blocks of all crochet projects and include the chain stitch, single crochet, double crochet, and treble crochet.

Chain Stitch

The chain stitch is the first stitch you'll learn in crochet. It forms a series of loops that can be used as a foundation for other stitches. To make a chain stitch, follow these steps:

1. Make a slip knot: To start, make a small loop with your yarn, and insert the hook through the loop from front to back. Pull the loose end of the yarn to tighten the loop around the hook. This is your slip knot.

2. Hold the hook: Hold the hook in your right hand like a pencil, with the hook facing up and the thumb and index finger holding the base of the hook.

3. Make a chain: Insert the hook into the slip knot from front to back, wrapping the yarn over the hook from back to front. Pull the yarn through the loop on the hook to create a new loop. This is your first chain stitch.

4. Continue: Keep making chain stitches by repeating step 3 until you have as many chains as you need for your project.

Single Crochet

The single crochet stitch is the simplest type of crochet stitch. It creates a dense fabric that is great for projects such as dishcloths and coasters. To make a single crochet, follow these steps:

1. Insert the hook: Insert the hook into the second chain from the hook, from front to back.

2. Yarn over: Wrap the yarn over the hook from back to front.

3. Pull through: Pull the hook and yarn through the chain, creating two loops on the hook.

4. Yarn over: Wrap the yarn over the hook from back to front.

5. Pull through both loops: Pull the hook and yarn through both loops on the hook, creating one loop.

6. Continue: Keep making single crochet stitches by repeating steps 1-5 for each chain stitch.

Double Crochet

The double crochet stitch creates a looser, lacy fabric than the single crochet stitch. It's a great stitch for making blankets, shawls, and scarves. To make a double crochet, follow these steps:

1. Yarn over: Wrap the yarn over the hook from back to front.

2. Insert the hook: Insert the hook into the second chain from the hook, from front to back.

3. Yarn over: Wrap the yarn over the hook from back to front.

4. Pull through: Pull the yarn through the chain, creating three loops on the hook.

5. Yarn over: Wrap the yarn over the hook from back to front.

6. Pull through two loops: Pull the hook and yarn through the first two loops on the hook, creating two loops.

7. Yarn over: Wrap the yarn over the hook from back to front.

8. Pull through two loops: Pull the hook and yarn through the last two loops on the hook, creating one loop.

9. Continue: Keep making double crochet stitches by repeating steps 2-8 for each chain stitch.

Treble Crochet

The treble crochet stitch is a tall stitch that creates a loose, lacy fabric. It's great for projects where you want a lot of drape or when you need to work up a project quickly. To make a treble crochet, follow these steps:

1. Yarn over twice: Wrap the yarn over the hook twice, from back to front.

2. Insert the hook: Insert the hook into the fourth chain from the hook, from front to back.

3. Yarn over: Wrap the yarn over the hook from back to front.

4. Pull through: Pull the yarn through the chain, creating four loops on the hook.

5. Yarn over: Wrap the yarn over the hook from back to front.

6. Pull through two loops: Pull the hook and yarn through the first two loops on the hook, creating three loops.

7. Yarn over: Wrap the yarn over the hook from back to front.

8. Pull through two loops: Pull the hook and yarn through the second and third loops on the hook, creating two loops.

9. Yarn over: Wrap the yarn over the hook from back to front.

10. Pull through two loops: Pull the hook and yarn through the last two loops on the hook, creating one loop.

11. Continue: Keep making treble crochet stitches by repeating steps 2-10 for each chain stitch.

Tips and Tricks for Crocheting Success

Now that you've learned the basic stitches, you're ready to start crocheting. Here are some tips and tricks to help you get the most out of your crochet projects:

1. Practice, practice, practice: Crochet takes time and practice to

master. Don't be discouraged if your first few projects don't turn out perfectly.

2. Use good lighting: Crochet can be hard on your eyes, so make sure you have good lighting when you're working.

3. Take breaks: Crochet can be addictive, but it's important to take breaks to stretch your hands and avoid injury.

4. Use stitch markers: Stitch markers can help you keep track of your progress and ensure that your stitches are even.

5. Block your finished projects: Blocking involves wetting your finished project and shaping it to the correct dimensions. This can make a big difference in the final appearance of your project.

6. Join a crochet community: Joining a crochet community can give you access to tips and advice from other crocheters, as well as a sense of camaraderie and support.

Crochet is a fun and rewarding hobby that can be enjoyed by people of all ages and skill levels. Whether you're a seasoned pro or a beginner, there's always something new to learn and create in the world of crochet. With the right supplies and some practice, you can start making beautiful and functional items that you'll be proud to show off to your friends and family. So grab your hooks and yarn, and let's get crocheting!

Chapter 2: History of Crochet

Crochet is a fantastic craft with a rich history that has remarkably evolved over time. In the 21st century, crochet continues to be a popular hobby for many people. Its origins can be traced back to the 19th century when it was primarily used as a means of creating lace and decorative fabrics. Throughout history, crochet has also been used to make practical items such as blankets, hats, socks, and shawls. In this chapter, we explore the fascinating history of crochet, its evolution, and how it has become a beloved art form around the world.

Origins of Crochet:

The invention of crochet is uncertain, as there is little documentation about how it came about. There are many theories about its origin, but the most widely accepted one is that it comes from China. This theory states that the Chinese first used a type of crochet in the 3rd century BC. As the story goes, a princess invented the technique as she was bored with traditional weaving methods. She took a long thin piece of bamboo and made tiny knots along it, creating a form of crochet.

Another theory suggests that crochet began in South America and the Caribbean. The women of these countries would create delicate lace using a crochet hook and fine thread. This process was known as "filet crochet," and it became popular during the 16th and 17th centuries.

Development of Crochet:

Crochet started to gain popularity in Europe during the 19th century. This was because of the increasing demand for lace and decorative fabric. With the advancement of technology, the production of lace was becoming more efficient, and crochet was becoming a beloved craft. Crochet started to spread throughout Europe, and different variations emerged in different countries.

In France, crochet was used as a way to create lace during the 1840s, where it was known as "tapestry crochet." This technique was different from the traditional crochet we know today. Rather than creating individual stitches in rows and rounds, the stitches were made in groups and worked in a diagonal direction. This technique was used to create tartan plaids and other colorful patterns.

In Ireland, crochet was used to create intricate motifs and edgings to add to fabrics that were already made. This was known as "Irish crochet," and it became popular in the late 19th and early 20th centuries. Irish crochet is unique in that it is made up of individual motifs that are joined together to make a larger fabric.

Crochet in America:

Crochet was becoming an increasingly popular hobby in America during the late 19th century. At this time, the women's magazine market was booming, and crochet patterns started to appear regularly in publications. This led to a vast growth in the popularity of crochet. During this period, women were making doilies, tablecloths, bedspreads, and other household items using crochet.

At the turn of the 20th century, crochet became more accessible to the masses as it became easier to obtain crochet hooks and yarn. With an abundance of available patterns, people were able to make a wide range of items. It was around this time that the first crochet magazines were published in America, catering to the growing interest in the craft.

Crochet during World War I:

During World War I, crochet played an important role in aiding the war effort. Soldiers and civilians alike were encouraged to crochet blankets and clothing for the troops. In 1917, the American Red Cross launched a nationwide "War Emergency" campaign that encouraged people to make blankets, socks, and other essential items using crochet. These were sent to Europe to aid the war effort.

Crochet in Modern Times:

Crochet has continued to evolve and grow in popularity throughout the 20th and 21st centuries. With the rise of social media, people have been able to share their love of the craft with others around the world. Online crochet communities and forums have developed, allowing crocheters to share patterns, techniques, and ideas with each other.

In addition to creating practical items like blankets and clothing, crochet has become a means of expression for many people. Artists have started using crochet as a form of installation art, creating large-scale pieces that are displayed in galleries and museums around the world. Crochet is also used to create sculptures and wall hangings, and it is a popular method of creating soft toys and dolls.

Crochet has a history that is rich and varied. For many, it is a beloved hobby that brings joy and satisfaction. It has evolved over time, adapting to the needs and desires of the people who practice it. From a basic practical skill used to create lace to a modern art form that is respected and celebrated around the world, the history of crochet continues to fascinate and inspire people today.

Chapter 3: Understanding Crochet Terminology

If you're new to crochet, the language surrounding the craft can be confusing. With so many different terms, abbreviations, and symbols, it's easy to feel overwhelmed. But don't worry – with a little bit of practice, you'll soon be speaking the language of crochet like a pro.

In this chapter, we'll explore some of the most common crochet terminology and explain what it all means. From basic stitches to advanced techniques, we'll cover everything you need to know to get started.

Basic Stitches

The foundation of any crochet project is the basic stitch. There are several different stitches you'll use regularly when crocheting, each with its own unique abbreviation. Here are the most common:

Chain Stitch (ch)

The chain stitch is the most basic stitch in crochet, and it's used to create the foundation chain that serves as the starting point for most projects. To create a chain stitch, simply loop the yarn over your hook and pull it through the loop already on your hook.

Single Crochet (sc)

The single crochet stitch is a simple stitch that forms a tight, dense fabric. To create a single crochet stitch, insert your hook into the next stitch, yarn over, and pull the yarn through the stitch. Then, yarn over again and pull through both loops on your hook.

Half Double Crochet (hdc)

The half double crochet stitch is essentially the same as the single crochet stitch, but with an extra step. To create a half double crochet stitch, yarn over your hook before inserting it into the next stitch, then follow the same steps as for a single crochet stitch.

Double Crochet (dc)

The double crochet stitch is a taller stitch that creates a more open and airy fabric than the single or half double crochet stitches. To create a double crochet stitch, yarn over before inserting your hook into the next stitch, then follow the same steps as for a single or half double crochet stitch.

Treble Crochet (tr)

The treble crochet stitch is even taller than the double crochet stitch, and it creates an even more open and airy fabric. To create a treble crochet stitch, yarn over twice before inserting your hook into the next stitch, then follow the same steps as for a single, half double, or double crochet stitch.

Advanced Techniques

As you become more comfortable with the basic stitches, you may want to try your hand at some more advanced techniques. Here are a few common ones to get you started:

Cluster Stitch

A cluster stitch is a group of two or more stitches worked into the same stitch or space to create a raised or bumpy texture. There are several different types of cluster stitches, but they all involve working multiple stitches together in some way.

Shell Stitch

A shell stitch is a grouping of multiple stitches worked into the same stitch or space to create a decorative edging. Typically, a shell stitch consists of several double crochet stitches worked into the same stitch or space.

Popcorn Stitch

A popcorn stitch is a type of cluster stitch that creates a raised, bobble-like texture. To create a popcorn stitch, work several double crochet stitches into the same stitch or space, then remove your hook from the last stitch and insert it into the top of the first stitch in the cluster. Grab the loop from the first stitch with your hook and pull it through the loop from the last stitch to create the popcorn.

Crochet Charts and Symbols

In addition to the written instructions for each stitch and technique, many crochet patterns also include charts or symbols that help to illustrate the pattern. These charts can be especially helpful if you're a visual learner or if you're working with a pattern that's written in a different language.

In a crochet chart, each stitch is represented by a symbol, and the chart itself shows the placement of each stitch in the pattern. Here are a few of the most common symbols you'll see in crochet charts:

- Chain stitch: a small, open circle
- Single crochet: a small "x"
- Half double crochet: a small "v"
- Double crochet: a tall "v"
- Treble crochet: a tall "y" or "7"

In addition to these basic symbols, there are also symbols that represent more complicated stitches and techniques, such as cluster stitches, shell stitches, and popcorn stitches.

Mastering the language of crochet takes time, but with a little bit of practice, you'll soon be speaking it like a pro. Remember to take it one stitch at a time, and don't be afraid to ask for help if you need it. With the right tools, techniques, and a little bit of patience, you'll be able to create beautiful crochet projects that you can be proud of.

Chapter 4: Choosing Your Crochet Hooks

Crocheting is a popular yet relaxing hobby enjoyed by millions of people worldwide. It involves creating exquisite fabrics and designs by interlocking loops of thread or yarn with a crochet hook. However, to perfect this craft, it is essential to choose the right crochet hooks that are comfortable, durable, and suit the project's requirements.

Crochet hooks are available in numerous types, sizes, and materials. Understanding the differences between each type is crucial for choosing the right tool for the job.

Types of Crochet Hooks

The most common types of crochet hooks available in the market include:

1. Straight hooks - These hooks are the most basic and inexpensive type of crochet hooks. They are perfect for starters as well as experienced crocheters.

2. Double-ended or Tunisian hooks - These hooks are longer than traditional straight hooks and have a hook on each end. They are ideal for creating larger projects like blankets or scarfs.

3. Interchangeable Hooks - These convenient hooks give you the

flexibility to switch hook sizes easily. They also save you money as you can purchase one set that has a variety of hook sizes instead of buying each separately.

4. Ergonomic hooks - These are specially designed to be more comfortable during long crocheting sessions. They have a handle that is easy to grip and reduce stress on the hands.

5. Steel hooks - These hooks have a tiny loop at the end and are used for fine crocheting projects like doilies, lace, or table runners.

Crochet Hook Sizes

Crochet hooks also come in various sizes. The sizes range from B (the smallest) to S (the largest), with letter and number sizes in between. The hook size chosen determines the gauge or tension of the stitches as well as the size of the finished project.

When starting your project, always ensure your hook size matches your yarn weight. If you are using bulky yarn, you need a larger hook size, and if you are using thin yarn, you need a smaller hook size.

Crochet Hook Materials

The crochet hooks vary in materials used, and each material has its own unique benefits. The most common materials include:

1. Aluminum - This is the most common material used in crochet hooks as it is inexpensive, lightweight, and durable.

2. Steel - These hooks are incredibly smooth and are perfect for fine crochet work.

3. Bamboo - Bamboo hooks are lighter than their aluminum and steel counterparts. They are heftier and can relieve strain on the hands.

4. Plastic - These are the lightest crochet hooks available and are perfect for beginners. They are also cost-effective and don't rust or corrode.

5. Wood - These hooks are heavier than the plastic counterparts, but they are made with the same techniques as bamboo hooks. They are ideal for those with hand arthritis.

Choosing The Right Crochet Hook

Choosing the right crochet hook can be challenging, but the ultimate choice will depend on your preference, comfort, skill level, and project requirements. Here are some guidelines to help you pick the right hook:

1. Consider your comfort - Ensure you choose a hook with a handle that fits comfortably in your hand. If you have arthritis or other conditions that affect your hand's movement, consider an ergonomic

hook that reduces hand pain and fatigue.

2. Proposed project - Consider the size of your project, the type of yarn you will be using, and the difficulty level of the project. For intricate work like lace or doilies, you may need fine steel hooks. For bulky projects that use thicker yarns like blankets, you may require a large hook.

3. Your experience level - As a beginner, you may not require specialized hooks. You will find a basic aluminum or plastic hook suitable. Intermediate and expert crocheters may need more specific hooks to add that level of specialty to their work.

4. Hook material - I prefer lightweight aluminum hooks, but if you prefer heftier hooks, you can opt for bamboo or wood. Steel hooks are ideal for those who prefer fine work.

5. Hook size - Ensure you choose the right hook size, as it determines your project's size. Always check the yarn label for the recommended hook size for the type of yarn you plan to use.

Choosing the right crochet hook is crucial for a successful and enjoyable crocheting experience. Select a hook that suits your skill level, project requirements, and comfort level. The hook material, size, and type are critical considerations that will determine the quality and finish of your project.

Ultimately, the choice of the perfect hook is a personal preference. It would help if you experimented with different hooks to find the one that meets all your requirements. With the right hook, you will enjoy crocheting, improve your skills, and create beautiful works of art.

Chapter 5: Understanding Yarn Weights and Types

Yarn is a fundamental element of any knitting or crochet project. It's what brings the vision of the designer to life, and it's what makes the difference between a professional-looking garment and an ill-fitted mess. Therefore, it's essential to understand the different types and weights of yarn available to ensure your project is a success.

Types of Yarn

Yarn is generally made of either animal fibers, plant fibers, or synthetics. Here are some common types of yarn:

1. Wool – One of the most popular natural fibers, wool is a warm, soft, and durable yarn. It comes from the fleece of sheep, goats, or llamas.

2. Cotton – Made from the fluffy fibers surrounding cotton seeds, cotton yarn is a lightweight, soft, and comfortable option for warm weather clothing.

3. Acrylic – A synthetic yarn made from polymer fibers, acrylic is a low-cost alternative to wool. It's typically lightweight, easy to care for, and comes in a wide range of colors.

4. Alpaca – Similar to wool, alpaca is a luxurious, soft, and warm fiber that comes from the alpaca animal.

5. Silk – A luxurious and shiny yarn, silk is a natural fiber that is lightweight and drapes beautifully. It's often blended with other fibers to add strength and texture.

Yarn Weights

Yarn weight refers to the thickness of the yarn strand. Here are the seven standard yarn weights:

1. Lace – The thinnest yarn weight, lace-weight yarn is used to create delicate, intricate designs. It's typically used with size US 000-1 (1.5-2.25mm) needles.

2. Fingering – Also known as sock weight yarn, fingering weight yarn is slightly thicker than lace weight yarn. It's a popular choice for socks, shawls, and lightweight garments and accessories. Fingering weight yarn is typically used with size US 1-3 (2.25-3.25mm) needles.

3. Sport – A lighter alternative to DK weight yarn, sport weight yarn is a versatile option. It's typically used for sweaters, socks, and other lightweight garments. Sport weight yarn is typically used with size US 3-5 (3.25-3.75mm) needles.

4. DK – DK weight yarn is a popular choice for a wide range of projects. It's slightly thicker than sport weight yarn and is commonly used for sweaters, hats, and scarves. DK weight yarn is typically used

with size US 5-7 (3.75-4.5mm) needles.

5. Worsted – One of the most commonly used yarn weights, worsted weight yarn is a versatile option. It can be used for a wide range of projects, including sweaters, blankets, and hats. Worsted weight yarn is typically used with size US 7-9 (4.5-5.5mm) needles.

6. Bulky – Bulky weight yarn is thicker than worsted weight yarn and is used to create quick and chunky projects like blankets and scarves. It's typically used with size US 9-11 (5.5-8mm) needles.

7. Super Bulky – The thickest yarn weight, super bulky yarn is used to create warm and cozy accessories like hats and scarves. It's typically used with size US 11 and up (8mm and up) needles.

When choosing yarn for your project, it's essential to consider both the yarn weight and type. The weight of the yarn will determine how your finished project will look, how it will drape, and how warm or cool it will be. The type of yarn will determine the texture and feel of the finished product.

Understanding yarn weights and types is crucial for knitting or crochet projects. It can make all the difference between a successful and beautiful finished product or a disappointing one. It's essential to choose the right yarn for your project to ensure that it meets your vision and the intended use of the item.

Chapter 6: How to Hold Your Crochet Hook

Crochet is a wonderful, relaxing hobby that many people enjoy. It allows you to create a wide variety of beautiful projects from blankets and scarves to clothing and home decor. One essential tool for crochet is the hook, which comes in various shapes and sizes. However, knowing how to hold your crochet hook correctly is just as important as picking the right one.

In this chapter, we'll cover the basics of how to hold your crochet hook, including different grips, hand positioning, and tips for reducing discomfort or hand strain. Whether you're a beginner or an experienced crocheter, learning how to hold your hook properly can improve your tension, speed, and confidence in your work.

The Grip:

Before we dive into hand positioning, let's talk about the grip. The way you hold your crochet hook will depend on personal preference and the project you're working on. Here are some of the most common grips:

1. Pencil Grip: Hold your hook as if you were writing with a pencil. This grip allows for precise movements and is ideal for intricate crochet work.

2. Knife Grip: Hold your hook as if you were holding a knife. This grip

allows for quick movements and is ideal for larger projects or when working with bulkier yarn.

3. Hybrid Grip: A combination of the pencil and knife grip. This grip is comfortable for many crocheters and allows for both precision and speed.

Hand Positioning:

Once you've decided on your grip, it's time to position your hand. Here are some tips to keep in mind:

1. Relax your hand: Crocheting with a tense hand can cause pain and discomfort. Try to keep your hand relaxed and free from tension.

2. Keep your wrist straight: Avoid bending your wrist while crocheting, as this can cause strain and discomfort. Keep your wrist straight and let your hand do most of the work.

3. Use your fingertips: Use your fingertips to control the hook and yarn. Avoid gripping the hook too tightly, as this can lead to tension in your hand and wrist.

4. Find your comfortable position: Everyone's hands are different, so find a position that is comfortable for you. You can hold the hook closer to the handle or further away, depending on what feels best.

Tips for Reducing Discomfort:

Crocheting for prolonged periods can cause discomfort and strain in your hands and wrists. Here are some tips to help reduce discomfort:

1. Take breaks: Take frequent breaks to stretch your hands and wrists. This will help prevent stiffness and soreness.
2. Use ergonomic hooks: There are many ergonomic crochet hooks available that are designed to reduce hand strain. Look for hooks with a comfortable grip, a smooth handle, and a shape that suits your grip style.

3. Use a comfortable chair: Sit in a comfortable chair with good back support. Avoid slouching or leaning forward, as this can cause strain in your neck and shoulders.
4. Exercise your hands: Regularly exercise your hands and wrists to keep them strong and flexible. You can try stretching, squeezing a stress ball, or using hand grips.

Learning how to hold your crochet hook correctly is essential for comfortable, efficient, and enjoyable crochet. Be sure to experiment with different grips and hand positions to find what works best for you. Remember to take frequent breaks and use ergonomic tools to prevent discomfort and strain. With practice and patience, you can master the art of crochet and create stunning projects that you are proud of.

Chapter 7: How to Hold Your Yarn

When you're first learning to knit or crochet, holding the yarn might seem like the most difficult part. However, with practice and patience, you'll quickly develop a technique that feels natural and comfortable. In this chapter, we'll explore different ways to hold your yarn and offer tips for improving your knitting or crocheting skills.

Before we get started, it's important to note that there's no one "right" way to hold your yarn. Every knitter and crocheter has their preferred style, and what works for one person may not work for another. It's important to experiment with different techniques and find what feels most comfortable for you.

The English Method

The English method, also known as the "throwing" method, involves holding the yarn in your right hand and "throwing" it over the needle or hook as you work. This method is often considered the easiest for beginners because it allows you to control the tension of the yarn more easily.

To hold the yarn using the English method:

1. Hold the end of the yarn with your left hand, allowing it to drape over your index and middle fingers.

2. Grip the yarn with your right hand by making a cup shape with your hand, using your thumb and first finger to hold the yarn.

3. Hold the needle or hook in your right hand, with the point facing your left hand.

4. Bring the needle or hook under the yarn in your left hand, from front to back.

5. "Throw" the yarn over the needle or hook with your right hand.

6. Pull the needle or hook through the loop to create a new stitch.

7. Repeat steps 4-6 as needed to create your desired pattern.

The Continental Method

The Continental method, also known as the "picking" method, involves holding the yarn in your left hand and "picking" it up with your right needle or hook. This method is popular in European knitting and produces a speedier knitting or crocheting pace.

To hold the yarn using the Continental method:

1. Hold the end of the yarn with your right hand, allowing it to drape over your index and middle fingers.

2. Grip the yarn with your left hand by making a cup shape with your hand, using your thumb and first finger to hold the yarn.

3. Hold the needle or hook in your right hand, with the point facing your left hand.

4. Bring the needle or hook from back to front, under the yarn in your left hand.

5. Use your right hand to "pick" the yarn up with the needle or hook.

6. Bring the right needle or hook over the left needle or hook and pull through the loop.

7. Repeat steps 4-6 as needed to create your desired pattern.

Other Techniques

There are many other ways to hold your yarn, and you may find that some of these work better for you than the English or Continental methods. Here are a few other techniques you can experiment with:

- The Portuguese method: This method involves wearing a pin or button on your shirt or lapel to anchor the yarn. The yarn is held in the left hand and "dropped" over the needle or hook with a flick of the thumb.

- The German or Combination method: This method is a combination of the English and Continental methods, using a combination of throwing and picking to create stitches.

- The Irish Cottage style: This method involves holding the yarn in both hands, with one end draped over the index finger of each hand. The left hand controls the tension, while the right hand "twists" the yarn over the needle or hook.

Tips for Success

No matter what method you use to hold your yarn, there are a few tips that can help you improve your knitting or crocheting skills:

1. Keep your tension consistent: Whether you're using the English, Continental, or another method, it's important to keep the tension of your yarn consistent throughout your work. Too much tension can make your stitches tight and difficult to work with, while too little tension can produce sloppy, loose stitches.

2. Use the right yarn for your project: Different yarns have different qualities that can affect their performance in a knitting or crocheting project. Be sure to choose a yarn that's appropriate for your project, and test it out before committing to a large project to ensure the yarn works well with your chosen method of holding.

3. Practice, practice, practice: The more you practice holding your

yarn, the more comfortable and natural it will feel. Try different techniques and projects to find what works best for you and don't be afraid to make mistakes – it's all part of the learning process!

Holding your yarn might take some practice and patience to master, but with the right technique and a little bit of practice, you'll be well on your way to becoming a skilled knitter or crocheter. Remember that everyone has their own preferred method, and there's no "right" or "wrong" way to hold your yarn – it's all about what works best for you. Whether you prefer the English, Continental, Portuguese, or another method, using these tips can help you improve your knitting or crocheting skills and create beautiful, professional-looking projects you can be proud of.

Chapter 8: Creating a Slipknot

A slipknot is often the very first step in most crochet projects. It is the initial loop on a hook that you start with before creating chains. Here's how you can create a slipknot for crochet:

Make a loop: Hold the end of the yarn in your right hand and wrap it around your left hand's fingers, from the back to the front, to create a loop.

Hold the yarn: With your right hand, grasp the yarn that's attached to the ball (not the end of the yarn). You want to hold it about 6-8 inches from the loop you just made.

Pull through: Push that piece of yarn through the loop, using your right fingers.

Create the knot: Hold onto the small loop (the one that was just pulled through the larger loop) with your left hand, and hold onto the end of the yarn (the shorter piece) with your right hand. Pull in opposite directions. The knot should slide up and tighten, but the loop will stay open. This is your slipknot.

Adjust the knot: Insert your crochet hook into the loop and hold the knot. Pull the long end of the yarn to make the loop smaller until it fits snugly on your hook.

You're ready to start crocheting! Make sure the knot is tight, but the loop is loose enough to move along the crochet hook. If you're right-handed, the knot should be on the hook in your right hand. If you're left-handed, the knot should be on the hook in your left hand.

This knowledge can add depth to your crochet projects and give you more confidence as you move beyond the basics. Here they are:

Understanding Yarn Labels: Yarn labels provide a lot of important information, including the yarn's weight, length, fiber content, recommended hook size, and care instructions. Learning how to interpret this information can help you choose the right yarn for your project.

Choosing the Right Crochet Hook: The size of the crochet hook you choose can significantly affect your project. The hook size influences the size of your stitches and, consequently, the drape and size of your final project. There's a standard set of crochet hook sizes, and your yarn label will often recommend a specific size.

Understanding Crochet Patterns: Crochet patterns can seem daunting at first with their abbreviations and terms. However, once you understand the basics, you'll be able to follow a pattern to create a wide range of items.

Learning Different Crochet Stitches: Beyond single and double crochet, there are many different stitches to learn, such as half-double crochet, treble crochet, and slip stitch. Each stitch has its own properties and uses. Some create a dense fabric, while others are more open and lacy.

Crochet Techniques: There are numerous techniques in crochet that allow you to add unique touches to your work. These include working in the round, creating granny squares, crocheting cables, and adding color changes.

Blocking Your Work: Once you've finished your crochet project, it may not look as neat as you'd like. Blocking is a technique that involves wetting your crochet piece and shaping it to the correct dimensions. It can make a significant difference, particularly for lace items or items that need to fit a specific size.

Caring for Crochet Items: Knowing how to care for your crochet items is important. This includes understanding washing and drying instructions, as well as how to store your crochet items when they're not in use.

Remember, like any craft, crochet is a skill that takes time and practice to master. Don't get discouraged if your first few attempts don't look perfect. Keep practicing, and you'll see improvement over time.

Chapter 9: Learning the Chain Stitch

The chain stitch is a basic crochet stitch that is often the first stitch beginners learn when starting out. Once mastered, it can be used to create a variety of different crochet projects, including scarves, blankets, and even clothing items.

If you are new to crochet, don't worry - the chain stitch is relatively easy to learn and perfect for beginners. In this chapter, we'll go through the basics of learning the chain stitch and provide some tips and tricks to help you get started.

Getting Started

Before you start crocheting, gather your supplies. You'll need a crochet hook, yarn, and scissors. Make sure the yarn you choose is appropriate for the crochet hook size you plan to use. You can find the recommended hook size on the yarn label.

To begin, create a slip knot in the yarn and place it on your crochet hook. Hold the crochet hook in your dominant hand and the yarn in your other hand. Keep the tension on the yarn by holding it between your fingers.

Step-by-Step Instructions

1. Hold the crochet hook in your dominant hand and the yarn in your

other hand.

2. Create a slip knot in the yarn and place it on your crochet hook.
3. Yarn over (wrap the yarn around the hook from back to front).
4. Pull the hook through the slip knot. You have just made your first chain stitch!
5. Repeat steps 3 and 4 until you have made the desired number of chain stitches.

Tips and Tricks

1. Keep your tension even. It's important to maintain an even tension throughout your crochet project to ensure that it turns out well. If your tension is too tight, it will be difficult to work with the yarn, and your project may end up stiff. If your tension is too loose, your stitches may not be uniform, and your project may not look as polished.

2. Count your stitches. It's easy to miscount your stitches, especially when you are just starting out. To avoid mistakes, count your stitches periodically as you work. This will help you catch any errors early on and make any necessary adjustments before you get too far along in your project.

3. Take breaks. Crocheting can be a lot of fun, but it can also be tiring on your hands and wrists. If you start to feel pain or discomfort, take a break and stretch your hands and fingers. It's also a good idea to practice good posture and take frequent breaks to avoid any strain

on your back and neck.

4. Experiment with different yarns and hook sizes. Yarn comes in a variety of textures, colors, and thicknesses. Experiment with different types of yarn and hook sizes to find what works best for you. Some yarns are easier to work with than others, and some hook sizes may produce a tighter or looser stitch depending on the yarn.

5. Don't be afraid to make mistakes. Crocheting is a learning process, and mistakes are a natural part of the process. If you make a mistake, don't be discouraged. Simply undo the stitches and try again. With practice, you'll improve your skills and become more comfortable with the process.

Learning the chain stitch is an important first step in mastering the art of crochet. With a few basic supplies and some practice, you can create beautiful crochet projects with ease. Remember to maintain an even tension, count your stitches, take breaks when necessary, experiment with different yarns and hook sizes, and don't be afraid to make mistakes. Happy crocheting!

Chapter 10: Learning the Single Crochet Stitch

Crocheting is a wonderful art that has been passed down for generations. It involves using a crochet hook and yarn to create patterns and designs. Crocheting is a great hobby that can help reduce stress, improve hand-eye coordination, and boost creativity. One stitch that is fundamental to crocheting is the single crochet stitch. In this chapter, we'll learn the basics of the single crochet stitch and how to make it.

Before we begin, remember that crocheting is not a race. It's important to take your time and enjoy the process. Don't worry if it takes a few tries to get the hang of the stitch. As you practice, your skills will improve, and you'll be creating beautiful projects before you know it.

Step 1: Choosing Your Yarn and Crochet Hook

The first step in learning the single crochet stitch is choosing the right materials. You'll need a crochet hook and some yarn. The size hook and yarn you choose will depend on your project and personal preference. A general rule of thumb is to use a smaller hook with thinner yarn and a larger hook with thicker yarn.

You'll also need to choose the color of yarn you want to use. Yarn comes in a wide variety of colors, so take your time and choose a color that you love. If you're new to crocheting, consider choosing a light-colored yarn. It will be easier to see your stitches as you work.

Step 2: Make a Slip Knot

Once you have your yarn and hook, you'll need to make a slip knot. The slip knot is the first stitch you'll make and will hold your yarn in place as you crochet. To make a slip knot, hold the end of your yarn in your left hand and drape the yarn over your right hand. Bring the end of the yarn over the top of the yarn and tuck it under the loop.

Next, use your hook to pull the yarn through the loop. Pull the yarn tight to create a knot. You now have a slip knot that you can use to start your project.

Step 3: Insert Your Hook

Before you can start making single crochet stitches, you'll need to insert your hook into the slip knot. To do this, hold your hook in your right hand and your slip knot in your left hand. Insert your hook into the center of the slip knot, from front to back.

Step 4: Yarn Over

The next step is to yarn over. Yarning over involves wrapping the yarn around your hook. To yarn over, bring your yarn over the top of your hook from back to front. Then, wrap the yarn over the top of the hook again from front to back.

Step 5: Pull Through

Once you've yarnt over, it's time to pull the yarn through the slip knot. Insert your hook into the slip knot, and pull the yarn through the loop. You now have two loops on your hook.

Step 6: Yarn Over Again

After you've pulled the yarn through the slip knot, you'll need to yarn over again. Bring the yarn over the top of your hook from back to front, and then wrap the yarn over the top of the hook again from front to back.

Step 7: Pull Through Both Loops

Now that you've completed the yarning over step, it's time to finish the single crochet stitch. Hold your two loops on your hook and pull the hook through both loops. You now have one loop on your hook, and you've completed your first single crochet stitch.

Step 8: Repeat the Process

To make more single crochet stitches, repeat the process. Insert your hook into the next stitch, yarn over, pull through, yarn over again, and pull through both loops.

As you practice the single crochet stitch, you'll start to develop a rhythm. You'll find that your fingers and hook will start to move more quickly, and you'll be able to complete stitches with ease.

Tips for Learning the Single Crochet Stitch

Learning a new stitch can be challenging, but with time and patience, you can master the single crochet stitch. Here are a few tips to help you along the way:

1. Use a smaller hook and lighter colored yarn when you're learning the stitch. It will be easier to see your stitches and prevent mistakes.
2. Practice the stitch on a small swatch before you start your project. It will help you get the hang of the stitch and avoid frustration.

3. Take breaks as needed. Crocheting can be relaxing, but it can also be tiring on your hands. Take a break when you need to prevent injury.

4. Don't worry about perfection. Remember that crocheting is an art, and imperfections give your project character.

Learning the single crochet stitch is a fundamental skill in crocheting. With practice and patience, you'll be able to make this stitch with ease and create beautiful projects. Remember to choose the right materials, take your time, and enjoy the process. As you work on your projects, you'll find that your skills improve, and you'll be able to tackle more complex stitches and designs.

Chapter 11: Learning the Double Crochet Stitch

Crocheting is a craft that has been around for centuries. It is a way of creating fabric using hook and yarn. There are many different stitches that you can use when you crochet, each with their own unique characteristics. One of the most popular crochet stitches is the double crochet stitch.

The double crochet stitch is a versatile stitch that can be used for many different projects. It creates a fabric that is dense and sturdy, making it perfect for blankets, scarves, and sweaters. The stitch is relatively easy to learn, even for beginners, and can be worked in rows or rounds.

Before you begin, you will need some basic supplies. You will need a crochet hook, yarn, and a pair of scissors. The size of your crochet hook will depend on the weight of your yarn. If you are using a thin yarn, you will need a smaller hook, and if you are using a thicker yarn, you will need a larger hook.

To begin, make a slip knot and place it on your hook. Next, chain a few stitches, depending on how wide you want your fabric to be. For this example, we will chain 10 stitches.

Next, yarn over your hook by wrapping the yarn around it from back to front. Insert your hook into the fourth chain from your hook.

Yarn over again and pull through the chain. You should now have three loops on your hook.

Yarn over again and pull through the first two loops on your hook. You should now have two loops on your hook.

Yarn over again and pull through the last two loops on your hook. You have now completed your first double crochet stitch!

Continue working double crochet stitches into each chain stitch across your row. When you reach the end of the row, turn your work and begin again.

Here are some tips for mastering the double crochet stitch:

1. Pay attention to tension. The tension of your stitches is important in creating a uniform fabric. Make sure you are not pulling too tightly or too loosely when you crochet.

2. Count your stitches. It's easy to lose track of how many stitches you've made, especially when you're just starting out. Counting your stitches at the end of each row will help ensure that your fabric is the correct width.

3. Use a stitch marker. If you are working in rounds, it can be helpful to use a stitch marker to keep track of where each round begins and ends. This will help you avoid mistakes and make it easier to count

your stitches.

4. Practice makes perfect. The more you practice the double crochet stitch, the easier it will become. Don't be discouraged if your first few attempts aren't perfect. Keep practicing and you will improve over time.

The double crochet stitch can be used in many different ways. Here are some ideas for incorporating this stitch into your projects:

1. Blankets: The double crochet stitch creates a dense and cozy fabric, making it perfect for blankets. You can create a simple striped blanket by alternating rows of different colors, or you can use the stitch to create a textured pattern.

2. Scarves: A scarf made with the double crochet stitch will be thick and warm, perfect for chilly winter days. You can create a simple straight scarf, or you can experiment with different stitch patterns to create a more complex design.

3. Sweaters: The double crochet stitch can be used to create a sturdy fabric for sweaters. You can create a simple pullover or cardigan, or you can use the stitch to create interesting texture and design elements.

4. Hats: A hat made with the double crochet stitch will be warm and cozy. You can create a simple beanie or slouchy hat, or you can

experiment with different stitch patterns to create a more unique design.

With a little bit of practice, the double crochet stitch can become a go-to stitch for all your crochet projects. Whether you're a beginner or an experienced crocheter, this versatile stitch is sure to be a favorite. So grab your hooks and yarn and start stitching!

Chapter 12: Learning the Treble Crochet Stitch

Crochet is one of the most fascinating and enjoyable needle crafts that people can take up. It can be used to create a wide range of items, from clothes, blankets, and baby items to household decorations and accessories. Many people start with the basics of single and double crochet stitches. Once these have been mastered, the next step is to progress onto the more advanced and complex stitches. One such stitch is the treble crochet stitch.

The treble crochet stitch is a tall stitch and is one of the taller stitches in the crochet world. It can create a beautiful and open-textured fabric, and is ideal for making lacy patterns, such as blankets, shawls, and scarves. Although it may seem daunting at first, once you have got the hang of it, you will find it an easy stitch to work, and will create some stunning works.

To begin, you will need a crochet hook and some yarn. Choose a yarn that is suitable for your project, and a hook that is appropriate for the yarn weight. For the treble crochet stitch, a hook size one or two sizes larger than the recommended size for the yarn is a good starting point.

Before you start, make sure you know how to create a chain stitch, as this is the basis for all crochet projects. Once you are confident with the chain stitch, you can move onto the first row of treble crochet.

The first step is to make a foundation chain. Create a chain that is a multiple of four stitches, plus one extra chain for turning. For this example, we will create a foundation chain of 21 stitches.

1. Make a slip knot and place it on your hook
2. Yarn over (wrap the yarn over your hook from back to front)
3. Insert the hook into the second chain from the hook
4. Yarn over and pull the yarn through the chain (you should now have three loops on your hook)
5. Yarn over, and pull through two loops on your hook. (You should now have two loops remaining on your hook)
6. Yarn over and pull through the remaining two loops. You have completed one treble crochet stitch.

7. To create the next treble crochet stitch, yarn over twice.
8. Insert your hook into the next chain stitch.
9. Yarn over and pull through the chain stitch (you should now have four loops on your hook)
10. Yarn over and pull through two loops on your hook.
11. Yarn over and pull through another two loops on your hook.
12. Yarn over and pull through the remaining two loops. You have completed the second treble crochet stitch.
13. Repeat steps 7-12 for every stitch in the chain.

Once you have completed the first row of stitches, you will need to turn your work. The turning chain counts as the first stitch of the next row. For the treble crochet stitch, the turning chain is four chains. To turn, chain four stitches, and then continue with the next row.

1. Yarn over twice
2. Insert your hook into the second stitch from the hook
3. Yarn over and pull through the stitch (you should have four loops on your hook)
4. Yarn over and pull through two loops on your hook.
5. Yarn over and pull through another two loops on your hook.
6. Yarn over and pull through the remaining two loops. You have completed your first treble crochet stitch of the second row.
7. Repeat steps 1-6 for every stitch in the row.

Keep repeating these steps until you have reached the desired length of your project. Once you have mastered the basic treble crochet stitch, there are many variations and techniques that you can use to create different textures and patterns.

Variations of the Treble Crochet Stitch

There are many variations of the treble crochet stitch that you can use to create different effects and textures. Here are some of the most popular.

Double Treble Crochet Stitch

The double treble crochet stitch is taller than the regular treble crochet stitch. To create a double treble crochet stitch, you need to yarn over three times before inserting your hook into the stitch.

1. Yarn over three times
2. Insert your hook into the stitch
3. Yarn over and pull through the stitch (you should have five loops on your hook)
4. Yarn over and pull through two loops on your hook.
5. Yarn over and pull through another two loops on your hook.
6. Yarn over and pull through another two loops on your hook.
7. Yarn over and pull through the remaining two loops. You have completed a double treble crochet stitch.

Half Treble Crochet Stitch

The half treble crochet stitch is shorter than the regular treble crochet stitch. It is a useful stitch to create a tighter fabric.

1. Yarn over
2. Insert your hook into the stitch
3. Yarn over and pull through the stitch (you should have three loops on your hook)
4. Yarn over and pull through all three loops on your hook. You have completed a half treble crochet stitch.

Front Post Treble Crochet Stitch

The front post treble crochet stitch is used to create a raised stitch that stands out from the fabric. It is an effective stitch that is often used in textured patterns.

1. Yarn over twice
2. Insert your hook from front to back and then to the front again around the post of the stitch you want to work into.
3. Yarn over and pull through the stitch (you should have four loops on your hook)
4. Yarn over and pull through two loops on your hook.
5. Yarn over and pull through another two loops on your hook.
6. Yarn over and pull through the remaining two loops. You have completed a front post treble crochet stitch.

Back Post Treble Crochet Stitch

The back post treble crochet stitch is similar to the front post treble crochet stitch, but it is worked around the back of the stitch instead of the front.

1. Yarn over twice
2. Insert your hook from back to front and then to the back again around the post of the stitch you want to work into.
3. Yarn over and pull through the stitch (you should have four loops on your hook)
4. Yarn over and pull through two loops on your hook.
5. Yarn over and pull through another two loops on your hook.

6. Yarn over and pull through the remaining two loops. You have completed a back post treble crochet stitch.

Learning the treble crochet stitch can open up a world of possibilities when it comes to crochet. With a bit of practice, you will find that it is an easy stitch to work, and can be used to create some stunning and intricate patterns. By using variations and combinations of the treble crochet stitch, you can create unique fabrics and textures that will be sure to impress. So why not give it a try and see what you can create? Happy crocheting!

Chapter 13: Learning the Half Double Crochet Stitch

The half double crochet stitch is a versatile crochet stitch that can be used in a variety of projects. It is shorter than a double crochet stitch but taller than a single crochet stitch. This makes it a great stitch for projects where you want a bit of height but not too much. In this chapter, we will explore how to properly execute the half double crochet stitch.

Getting Started

Before we dive into learning the half double crochet stitch, let's take a quick overview of the basic tools and materials you'll need to get started. You will need:

- Crochet hooks
- Yarn
- Scissors
- Tapestry needle

Let's talk about each of those briefly.

Crochet hooks: There are many different sizes of crochet hooks on the market, ranging from size 0.6 mm all the way up to size 25 mm. For most projects, you will want somewhere in the middle. A good rule of thumb is to choose a hook size that corresponds to the weight of the yarn you are using. For example, if you are using a worsted weight yarn, you will likely want to use a size H/8 (5 mm) hook.

Yarn: The type of yarn you choose will depend on the project you are working on. A basic worsted weight yarn is a good choice for beginner projects. As you become more comfortable with crochet, you can explore other yarn weights and types.

Scissors: You will need a good pair of scissors for cutting your yarn.

Tapestry needle: A tapestry needle is a long, blunt needle used for weaving in ends and seaming pieces together.

With these tools and materials in hand, you're ready to start learning the half double crochet stitch.

Step-By-Step Instructions

To begin, make a foundation chain of the desired length. If you're not familiar with how to make a chain, check out the "How to Crochet a Chain Stitch" chapter.

Once you have your foundation chain, yarn over (wrap the yarn over the hook) from back to front, then insert the hook into the third chain from the hook.

Yarn over again, then draw the yarn through the chain stitch.

You should now have three loops on your hook.

Yarn over again and draw the yarn through all three loops on the hook.

Congratulations! You've just completed your first half double crochet stitch.

To make additional stitches, simply repeat steps 2-5 for each stitch. When you reach the end of the row, chain two and turn your work. This will create the height necessary for the next row of stitches.

Troubleshooting

As with any new skill, it's possible that you may encounter some difficulties when learning the half double crochet stitch. Here are some common problems and solutions:

Problem: Stitches are too loose or too tight.

Solution: Check your tension. Make sure you're not pulling too tightly or not tightly enough. Also, make sure you're using the correct hook size for your yarn.

Problem: Stitches are uneven.
Solution: Make sure you're inserting the hook into the same part of the stitch for each stitch. It's easy to accidentally insert the hook into

the wrong spot, which can create uneven stitches.

Problem: Stitches are twisted.
Solution: Make sure you're not twisting your foundation chain before you start making stitches. Your chain should lay flat before you begin the next row of stitches.

Where to Use the Half Double Crochet Stitch
Now that you've learned how to make the half double crochet stitch, let's talk about some of the many ways you can use this versatile stitch.
Scarves: A scarf made with half double crochet stitches has a nice drape and texture. It's also a relatively quick project to make.
Blankets: Because the half double crochet stitch is taller than a single crochet stitch, it's a great option for making blankets. A blanket made with half double crochet stitches will be warm and cozy.
Hats: Depending on the weight of the yarn you choose, a hat made with half double crochet stitches can be lightweight and breathable or warm and cozy.

Bags: The half double crochet stitch creates a sturdy fabric, which makes it a good choice for bags and purses.

The half double crochet stitch is a versatile and easy-to-learn stitch that can be used in a variety of projects. With the proper tools and materials, you can get started on learning and mastering this stitch today. So grab your crochet hook and some yarn and give it a try!

Chapter 14: Learning to Increase and Decrease

Sure, increasing and decreasing in crochet is a fundamental skill that allows you to shape your work, whether that's creating a flat circle, a hat, an amigurumi toy, or a garment.

Increasing

Increasing is simply adding more stitches to your row than were in the previous row. It's typically done by making more than one crochet stitch into one stitch from the previous row.

Here's how you can increase in single crochet (abbreviated as "inc"):

Insert your hook into the stitch where you want to increase.

Yarn over and pull up a loop.

Yarn over again and pull through both loops on your hook. This is a regular single crochet stitch.

Now, into the same stitch, repeat the steps. Insert your hook, yarn over, pull up a loop, yarn over, pull through both loops. Now you've made two stitches where there was only one before, creating an increase.

For double crochet (abbreviated as "dc inc"), it's similar:

Yarn over, insert your hook into the stitch where you want to increase.

Yarn over and pull up a loop. You should have three loops on your hook.

Yarn over and pull through the first two loops. Yarn over again and pull through the last two loops.

In the same stitch, repeat the steps to make another double crochet.

This method can be adapted to any type of stitch. Always remember: an increase means more stitches in the current row than there were in the previous one.

Decreasing

Decreasing is the opposite of increasing. You're reducing the number of stitches from the previous row. It's typically done by combining two or more stitches from the previous row into one stitch.

Here's how you can decrease in single crochet (abbreviated as "sc dec" or "sc2tog"):

Insert your hook into the stitch where you want to decrease.

Yarn over and pull up a loop.

Then, insert your hook into the next stitch.

Yarn over and pull up a loop again. You should have three loops on your hook.

Yarn over and pull through all three loops on your hook.

Now you've made one stitch out of two, creating a decrease.

For a double crochet decrease (abbreviated as "dc dec" or "dc2tog"):

Yarn over, insert your hook into the first stitch you want to decrease, yarn over and pull up a loop, then yarn over and pull through two loops on your hook. You should have two loops remaining on your hook.

Yarn over, insert your hook into the next stitch, yarn over and pull up a loop, then yarn over and pull through two loops on your hook. Now, you should have three loops on your hook.

Yarn over and pull through all three loops.

In this case, you've turned two stitches into one, resulting in a decrease.

Once you master increasing and decreasing, you'll be able to tackle a wider variety of crochet projects as these techniques are widely used in shaping different pieces. Keep practicing, and you'll get the hang of it!

Chapter 15: Understanding Crochet Patterns

Crochet is a beautiful and versatile craft that has been enjoyed by people for centuries. It is a rewarding hobby that offers endless possibilities for creating unique and beautiful pieces, whether for personal use or as gifts for loved ones. However, for many beginners, crochet patterns can be confusing and intimidating. In this chapter, we will take a closer look at crochet patterns and offer tips and advice to help you understand and make the most of them.

1. The importance of reading the pattern

The first step to successfully creating a crochet project is understanding the pattern. Reading the pattern carefully before you start will ensure that you have all the necessary materials and are familiar with all the stitches you will need. A good pattern will provide you with a detailed list of materials, the number of stitches you need to work, and any abbreviations or special instructions you need to know.

2. Understanding the abbreviations

Crochet patterns often use abbreviations to make them easier to read and write. However, these abbreviations can be confusing for beginners who are not familiar with them. Here are some of the most common crochet abbreviations you are likely to encounter in a pattern:

· Ch – chain

· Sc – single crochet

· Dc – double crochet

· Tr – treble crochet

· Sl st – slip stitch

· Hdc – half double crochet

· Rep – repeat

· Inc – increase

· Dec – decrease

· Sts – stitches

3. Choosing the right yarn

Choosing the right yarn for your project is crucial. The pattern will usually specify the weight and type of yarn needed. There are many different types of yarn available, from lightweight cotton to thicker wool blends. It's important to choose a yarn that is appropriate for your project, in terms of both weight and texture. Crochet hooks also come in different sizes, so be sure to choose one that is appropriate for your yarn.

4. Understanding gauge

Gauge is the number of stitches and rows per inch that are worked with a particular yarn and hook size. Understanding gauge is important because it can affect the size and fit of your finished project. A pattern will often specify a gauge to aim for, and it's important to work with a test swatch before beginning your project to ensure that your gauge matches the pattern.

5. Following the instructions

Once you've read the pattern and gathered your materials, it's time to start crocheting. It's important to follow the instructions carefully, especially when it comes to stitch counts and shaping. Even small deviations from the pattern can dramatically affect the finished product. If you get stuck, there are many online resources available, including YouTube tutorials and crochet forums, where you can ask for help.

6. Tips for beginners

If you're new to crochet, there are a few tips that can help you master the craft:

· Start small: Begin with simple projects that use basic stitches, such as scarves, dishcloths, or coasters.

· Practice: Like any skill, crochet takes practice. The more you practice, the more confident you will become.

· Use stitch markers: Stitch markers can help you keep track of where you are in a pattern and save you time and frustration.

· Take breaks: Crochet can be time-consuming and physically demanding. Take breaks when you need to, and don't push yourself too hard.

7. Common mistakes to avoid

Even experienced crocheters make mistakes, but there are some common errors that beginner often make:

· Incorrect stitch count: Missing or adding stitches can affect the size and shape of your project.

· Tension issues: Crochet stitches can become too tight or too loose, affecting the finished product.

· Not weaving in ends: Leaving loose ends can make your project look messy and unfinished.

· Giving up too easily: Crochet can take time and patience, so don't let mistakes or setbacks discourage you.

Understanding crochet patterns is an essential part of mastering this beautiful craft. By following the tips and advice outlined in this chapter, you can gain confidence and enjoy the many benefits of crochet. Whether you're creating a beautiful afghan or a simple dishcloth, crochet is a rewarding hobby that can provide you with a lifetime of enjoyment. Happy crocheting!

Chapter 16: Reading Crochet Diagrams

Crochet diagrams, also known as chart or schematic patterns, offer an alternative to written patterns for those who prefer visual aids when crocheting. While some experienced crocheters may find written patterns to be more convenient, diagrams are extremely helpful for beginners as they depict each stitch and its placement in a clear and concise manner. In this chapter, we will explore the benefits of using crochet diagrams, how to read them, and the various symbols used in them.

Benefits of Using Crochet Diagrams

Crochet diagrams offer a number of benefits that make them a popular choice among crocheters. One of the most significant advantages of using crochet diagrams is that they are visual aids that enable beginners to easily understand the pattern. Written patterns can be challenging for starters to comprehend, especially if they are not familiar with the terminologies used in the pattern. The visual representation of the crochet stitches in diagrams helps a beginner to better understand the pattern, the placement, and the number of stitches required to create a certain design. Crochet diagrams are also helpful for people who have disabilities with reading and writing such as dyslexia since they only require visual interpretation.

Secondly, crochet diagrams are much easier to follow, especially for patterns with intricate stitch-work, color changes, or multiple stitch combinations. The diagrams are clear, concise, and give a clear picture of how the stitches should be worked, making the pattern much simpler to follow. This helps to prevent errors and mistakes that may arise when crocheting from written patterns, especially if the crochet pattern language is not well understood.

Thirdly, crochet diagrams eliminate language barriers between crocheters who speak different languages. The crochet symbols used in the diagrams are universal, making it easy for anyone to understand and follow the pattern. This convenience means that a crocheter can follow a pattern from a pattern book or an online pattern, even if they do not speak the language in which the pattern was written. This makes it easy for crocheters to connect and share their craft with other crocheters from across the globe.

How to Read Crochet Diagrams

Reading a crochet diagram may look daunting for a beginner, but once the basics are grasped, it becomes easy to follow. Generally, crochet diagrams are read from the bottom up, from right to left. This means that you begin with the first row at the bottom of the chart and work your way up to the last row at the top of the chart. The first stitch of each row is at the right edge of the chart, and the last stitch is at the left edge.

Before getting started with reading a crochet diagram, it is important to understand the symbols and abbreviations used in the diagram.

The chart key on the pattern will have the corresponding symbols for the stitches used in the pattern. One of the most important symbols used in crochet diagrams is the dot. This symbol indicates the placement of the stitch, while the horizontal line shows the direction of the stitch that should be worked.

Once you have familiarized yourself with the symbols, you can begin reading the chart. The first row of the chart represents the first row of the pattern. Each block on the chart represents a single stitch. To begin, simply locate the first block on the first row of the chart, which represents the first stitch on the first row of the pattern. Determine the stitch symbol of the block and work the corresponding stitch, following the horizontal line to determine the direction of the stitch. Continue working the stitches in order, row by row, to complete the pattern.

It is essential to keep a keen eye on the symbols and the positioning of the stitches while working with crochet diagrams. Errors and mistakes can easily occur if the symbols or placement are misinterpreted or missed. It is always advisable to have a hard copy of the pattern close by to refer to for guidance.

Symbols Used in Crochet Diagrams

As mentioned earlier, crochet diagrams contain a chart key that provides a guide to the symbols and abbreviations. Understanding the symbols is crucial for working on a crochet pattern as they indicate the placement and type of stitch to be worked. Here are some of the symbols that may appear on a crochet diagram:

Chain Stitch (ch): The chain stitch is represented by a vertical line with a loop on top. This symbol indicates the position of the chain stitch in the pattern.

Single Crochet Stitch (sc): The shallow "v" symbol represents the single crochet stitch. The symbol indicates where the single crochet stitch should be placed.

Half-Double Crochet Stitch (hdc): The half-double crochet stitch is represented by a horizontal line with a vertical line at the center. The symbol indicates where the middle or third loop of the half-double crochet stitch should be placed.

Double Crochet Stitch (dc): The double crochet stitch is represented by a sideways "V." The tall and triangular shape of the symbol indicates where the double crochet stitch should be placed.

Treble Crochet Stitch (tr): The treble crochet stitch is represented by a vertical line with a horizontal line passing through it and a small triangle on top of the line. The symbol indicates where the treble crochet stitch should be placed.

Slip Stitch (sl st): The slip stitch is represented by a small dot. The symbol indicates the placement of the slip stitch.

Crochet diagrams are a great alternative to written patterns for those who prefer visual aids while crocheting. They are especially helpful for beginners or those who struggle with written patterns, and also for those who may not speak the language in which the pattern is written. Reading crochet diagrams may seem daunting at first, but through practice, it becomes easier and less intimidating. Understanding the symbols used in the crochet diagrams is crucial when working on a pattern. Through mastering crochet diagrams, crocheters can create intricate designs with ease, while enjoying the benefits of using visual aids.

Chapter 17: How to Finish a Crochet Project

Crocheting is a popular pastime enjoyed by people of all ages and skill levels. From simple projects like dishcloths and scarves to elaborate creations like blankets and clothing, crochet offers endless possibilities for creativity and self-expression.

But once you've completed your project, what's next? How do you finish it off and ensure that it's ready to be used or displayed? In this chapter, we'll explore the steps involved in finishing a crochet project and offer tips and tricks to help you get the best results.

Blocking

The first step in finishing a crochet project is blocking. This process involves wetting the item and shaping it to the desired size and shape. Blocking helps even out any uneven stitches, correct any curling or rolling, and give the finished product a more polished look.

To block a crochet project, you'll need a flat surface, some rustproof pins, and a spray bottle filled with water. Start by laying the item out on the flat surface and pinning it into place, making sure to stretch the fabric evenly and smooth out any bumps or lumps.

Once you've pinned the item into place, use the spray bottle to wet the fabric and let it dry completely. This could take several hours or even overnight, depending on the size of the project and the humidity levels in your area.

Weaving in Ends

Once your project has been blocked and is dry, the next step is to weave in any loose ends. This is important for both aesthetic reasons and practical reasons - loose ends can get caught on things or cause the project to unravel.

To weave in ends, you'll need a yarn needle and a pair of scissors. Simply thread the needle with the loose end of the yarn and weave it in and out of the stitches on the backside of the project. Take care to ensure that the end is secure and won't come loose over time.

If you have a lot of ends to weave in, it can be helpful to plan ahead and weave them in as you go. For example, if you're making a stripey blanket, you can weave in the ends of each color as you switch to the next one. This can make the finishing process much more manageable.

Adding Edgings

Adding an edging to your crochet project can help give it a more finished look and can also be a fun way to add a pop of color or texture. There are many different types of edgings you can choose from, including simple single crochet, picot, scallop, or shell edgings.

To add an edging, you'll need to decide on the type of edging you want to use and choose a complementary color of yarn. You'll also need a crochet hook that is appropriate for the weight of your yarn.

Start by attaching the yarn to a corner or seam of your project, then work your way around the edge, making stitches evenly spaced apart. You may need to adjust the number of stitches you make depending on the shape of your project - for example, you might need to make more stitches on a curved edge than on a straight edge.

Once you've worked your way around the entire edge, join the last stitch to the first one and tie off the yarn. Take care to ensure that the edging is even and neat, with no puckering or bunching.

Washing and Blocking Again

If you've added an edging to your project, it's a good idea to wash it again before use or display. This will help remove any dirt or oils that may have accumulated during the finishing process and will also help the fabric to relax and settle into its final shape.

To wash your crocheted item, fill a sink or basin with cool water and add a small amount of gentle detergent. Gently agitate the item in the water, taking care not to stretch or twist it, then rinse it thoroughly and gently press out any excess water.

Once your item is clean and wet, you can block it again to ensure it maintains its shape and size. Follow the same blocking process as before, making sure to stretch and shape the fabric evenly and smooth out any bumps or lumps.

Storing Your Project

Once your crochet project is finished and dry, it's important to store it properly to ensure it stays looking its best. Here are some tips for storing your crochet projects:

- Fold items neatly and stack them in a drawer or on a shelf.
- Hang items on hangers with padded clips to avoid stretching or distorting the fabric.
- Store items in acid-free tissue paper or garment bags to protect them from dust and dirt.
- Avoid storing items in direct sunlight or in damp environments, as this can cause fading or mildew.

By following these simple steps, you can ensure that your crochet projects look their best and last for years to come. So go ahead and tackle that next project with confidence, knowing that you have the skills to finish it off like a pro.

Chapter 18: Blocking Your Crochet Projects

Crochet is one of the most popular and rewarding hobbies in the world, and for good reason. Not only does it allow people to create beautiful and practical items for themselves, but it can also be incredibly therapeutic and relaxing. However, even the most experienced crocheters can run into problems when it comes to blocking their finished projects. In this chapter, we will delve into the ins and outs of blocking your crochet projects, including what it is, why it's important, and how to do it properly.

What Is Blocking?

Blocking is the process of manipulating your finished crochet item after it has been completed. This can involve stretching, shaping, and even dampening the fibers in order to achieve the desired size and shape. In some cases, blocking may also involve adding additional embellishments or details, such as buttons or pom-poms.

Why Is Blocking Important?

Blocking is important for a number of reasons. First and foremost, it can help to ensure that your finished project looks and fits exactly the way you want it to. Without blocking, your crochet item may be misshapen or not the correct size, which can be frustrating and disappointing.

Additionally, blocking can also help to even out any irregularities or bumps that may have occurred during the crocheting process. This can be especially important for projects that involve intricate stitches or patterns.

Finally, blocking can also help to add some extra polish and professionalism to your finished project. By taking the time to block your item properly, you can help to ensure that it looks its best and reflects the time and effort you put into creating it.

How to Block Your Crochet Project:

Now that we know why blocking is important, let's take a closer look at how to actually do it. Here are some steps to follow:

Step 1: Gather Your Supplies

Before you begin blocking your crochet project, you will need to gather a few supplies. These may include:

- A basin or sink
- A towel
- Pins
- Measuring tape
- A blocking board

Step 2: Wet Your Project

In order to properly block your crochet project, you will need to get it wet. This can be done by either immersing it in a basin or sink full of water, or by wetting it down with a spray bottle.

Once your project is wet, it is important to gently squeeze out any excess water. You can do this by rolling it up in a towel and pressing down gently, or by simply squeezing it between your hands.

Step 3: Pin Your Project

Next, it's time to start pinning your project. This involves using special blocking pins to shape and stretch your item into the desired shape and size.

Begin by laying your crochet item out on a flat surface. You can use a blocking board or other flat surface for this.

Next, use your pins to pull the fabric into the correct shape. For example, if you are blocking a sweater, you may want to stretch the sleeves out slightly to make them a bit longer.

Be sure to take your time with this process, as it is important to get the shape and size of your project just right.

Step 4: Allow Your Project to Dry

Once your project is pinned out into the desired shape, it's time to let it dry completely. This can take several hours or even overnight, depending on the size and thickness of your item.

It is important to allow your project to dry completely before unpinning it, as this will help to ensure that it retains its shape.

Step 5: Unpin Your Project

Once your project is completely dry, it's time to remove the pins and see your finished result! Be sure to carefully remove the pins without snagging or damaging your crochet item.

Step 6: Enjoy Your Finished Project!

Congratulations, you have successfully blocked your crochet project! Take some time to admire your handiwork and enjoy your finished creation.

Blocking your crochet projects can be a time-consuming and somewhat daunting task, but it is an essential step in ensuring that your finished items look and fit exactly the way you want them to. By following the steps outlined above, you can help to ensure that your crochet projects always look their best, and that your hard work pays off in the end. So go forth and create, knowing that your items will be perfectly sized and shaped thanks to the power of blocking!

Chapter 19: Troubleshooting Common Crochet Problems

Crochet is a craft that involves creating a fabric using yarn and a crochet hook. The technique involves pulling loops of the yarn through other loops on the hook to create a pattern. While crochet can be a fun and relaxing hobby, it can also be frustrating when things go wrong. In this chapter, we will discuss some of the most common crochet problems and how to troubleshoot them.

Problem 1: Tangled Yarn

Tangled yarn can be a nightmare for any crocheter. It's distracting, time-consuming, and frustrating. The best way to prevent yarn tangling is to use a yarn bowl. Yarn bowls come in different sizes, shapes, and materials, but they all serve the same purpose: keeping the yarn ball stationary while you crochet. If you don't have a yarn bowl, you can create your own by placing the yarn ball in a clean bowl or container and threading the yarn through a small hole or notch on the side.

If your yarn is already tangled, don't panic. The first step is to stop crocheting and evaluate the situation. Take note of where the tangles are and start untangling from the outside in. Avoid pulling on the yarn too hard, as it can make the tangles worse. Instead, turn the ball upside down and let the tangled section hang while gently pulling on the untangled section. Repeat until the tangles are removed.

Problem 2: Uneven Tension

Crochet requires consistent tension to achieve a uniform appearance. Uneven tension can cause stitches to be too tight or too loose, resulting in an uneven or warped finished project. Improving your tension takes practice and patience, but there are a few tips that can help.

First, make sure that you're holding the yarn and hook correctly. Your grip should be loose and relaxed, with the hook held like a pencil and the yarn draped over your fingers. Next, try to keep your tension consistent throughout the project. You can do this by monitoring your stitches and adjusting your grip accordingly, or by using a tensioning device like a yarn guide.

If you're still having trouble with uneven tension, try using a different hook size or yarn weight. Sometimes a simple change can make a big difference. You can also try blocking your finished project to even out any tension issues.

Problem 3: Miscounted Stitches

Miscounting stitches is a common mistake in crochet, and it can be frustrating to unravel rows of work to fix a mistake. The best way to avoid miscounting is to use stitch markers. Stitch markers are small pieces of plastic or metal that you can place in your work to mark a specific stitch or section. You can use different colors or shapes to represent different types of stitches or pattern repeats.

If you do miscount, don't panic. Depending on the mistake, you may be able to fudge the stitch count without anyone noticing. For example, if you're working a ripple pattern and you end up with an extra or missing stitch, you can simply increase or decrease the stitch count in the next row to compensate.

If the mistake is too significant to ignore, you may need to unravel some rows to get back to the correct stitch count. To make this process easier, try writing down each row as you complete it, noting the stitch count at the beginning and end of each row.

Problem 4: Yarn Splitting

Yarn splitting is when the yarn separates into individual strands, making it difficult to work with. This is a common problem with loosely spun or silky yarns, but it can happen with any type of yarn. To avoid yarn splitting, try using a different hook size or yarn weight. You can also try using a crochet hook with a smaller or blunter tip, which will catch the yarn less.

If your yarn is already splitting, try moistening it slightly with a spray bottle or a damp cloth. This can help the fibers stick together and prevent further splitting. You can also try inserting your hook into the middle of the yarn strand, rather than the edge, so that the strands stay together.

Problem 5: Uneven Edges

Uneven edges are a common problem in crochet, especially for beginners. There are a few reasons why this might happen, including uneven tension or inconsistent stitch size. To prevent uneven edges, make sure that you're beginning each row in the correct place, and that your stitches are evenly spaced.

If you're still having trouble, try using a turning chain at the beginning of each row. A turning chain is a chain stitch that you work at the beginning of each row to bring your hook to the correct height for the next row. The number of turning chains you need to work depends on the height of the stitch you're using. For example, if you're working double crochets, you'll need to work two turning chains at the beginning of each row.

Crochet is a fun and accessible craft, but it does have its challenges. By troubleshooting common problems like tangled yarn, uneven tension, miscounted stitches, yarn splitting, and uneven edges, you can improve your skills and create beautiful projects. Remember to take your time, be patient, and don't be afraid to try new techniques. Happy crocheting!

Chapter 20: Understanding Gauge in Crochet

Understanding gauge in crochet is of paramount importance if you want to create beautiful and professional-looking projects. Gauge refers to the number of stitches and rows you need to create in a specific pattern using a particular hook size and yarn weight to obtain the correct dimensions and tension of your finished work.

In simple words, gauge is a measure of how tight or loose your crochet stitches are and determines the size and fit of your finished project. Crochet gauges can vary significantly from person to person, so it's essential to find the right combination of hook size, yarn weight, and stitch pattern for your project.

In this chapter, we'll cover the basics of understanding gauge, including how to measure your gauge, what factors affect gauge, the different types of stitch patterns, and how to adjust your tension to get the perfect gauge.

Measuring Gauge

Measuring your gauge is a crucial step in crocheting a project that fits perfectly and looks good. To measure your gauge, you'll need to crochet a swatch of sample stitches in the pattern you'll be using.

The swatch should be at least 4"x 4" and have enough stitches and rows to give an accurate representation of the stitch pattern. You can use any yarn and hook size you prefer, as long as it is close to the one specified in the pattern.

Once you've completed your swatch, place it on a flat surface and measure the stitches and rows. Take care to measure the gauge in the middle of the swatch to ensure the right fit and size.

Ideally, the gauge in your swatch should match the gauge specified in your pattern. If you have too many stitches and rows in your swatch, your gauge is too tight, and you need to use a larger hook size and looser tension. Conversely, if you have too few stitches and rows, your gauge is too loose, and you need to use a smaller hook size and tighter tension.

Factors Affecting Gauge

Several factors influence the gauge in your crocheting projects, including hook size, yarn weight, stitch pattern, and even your tension or crocheting style.

Hook Size

Different crochet hook sizes produce different gauges and stitch sizes. A smaller hook size creates tighter stitches, while a larger hook size creates looser stitches. Knowing the correct hook size for your pattern is vital, as changing the hook size can significantly affect the final size and fit of your project.

Yarn Weight

Yarn weight refers to the thickness and texture of the yarn you use in your projects. Heavier yarns create larger stitches and looser gauges, while lighter yarns create tighter stitches and smaller gauges.

It's important to choose the right yarn weight for your pattern and hook size. Some crochet patterns recommend specific yarn weight and hook sizes in combination, so make sure to follow the instructions carefully.

Stitch Pattern

Different stitch patterns require different tensions and hook sizes to achieve the correct gauge. For example, a dense, textured stitch like the bobble stitch will result in a smaller gauge than a simpler stitch like single crochet.

When selecting your stitch pattern, be aware that more intricate stitches may require more practice and experimentation to achieve the correct gauge.

Adjusting Tension

Adjusting your tension or crocheting style is another important factor in crocheting the perfect gauge. Tension refers to the amount of pressure you apply to your yarn as you crochet, and it impacts the size and tightness of your stitches.

If you're consistently creating too many stitches and rows in your swatch, you need to loosen your tension. To do this, try relaxing your grip and focusing on making more natural, fluid movements with your hook.

Alternatively, if you're not creating enough stitches and rows, you need to tighten your tension. To do this, try increasing the pressure on your yarn, creating smaller and tighter stitches.

Types of Stitch Patterns

The type of stitch pattern you use in your project can affect the gauge and final size of your work. Some patterns, like single or double crochet, create uniform, neat stitches that are easy to adjust to the correct gauge. Others, like the shell stitch, require more practice and experimentation to achieve the correct gauge.

Single Crochet

Single crochet is one of the most commonly used stitch patterns in crocheting. It creates tight, uniform stitches that are easy to adjust to the correct gauge. Single crochet stitches are typically shorter and thinner, making them perfect for creating small projects like coasters and dishcloths.

Double Crochet

Double crochet is another popular stitch pattern that creates slightly larger and looser stitches than single crochet. It's perfect for creating blankets, shawls, and other larger projects that require a looser stitch.

Half-Double Crochet

Half-double crochet is a combination of single crochet and double crochet, creating slightly shorter and tighter stitches than double crochet. It's perfect for creating more substantial, thicker projects like scarves and beanies.

Shell Stitch

The shell stitch is a beautiful, textured stitch pattern that creates rows of fan-shaped shells. It's perfect for creating blankets, shawls, and other entire projects that require a delicate touch.

Understanding gauge is an essential skill in crocheting projects that fit perfectly and look good. Measuring your gauge, knowing the factors that affect gauge, adjusting your tension, and selecting the right stitch pattern are all crucial steps in achieving your desired gauge.

By following the tips, tricks, and techniques outlined in this chapter, you can easily master gauge and achieve the perfect fit in all your crocheting projects. Keep practicing and experimenting with different yarns, hook sizes, and stitch patterns until you find the perfect combination for your next masterpiece.

Chapter 21: Crochet Project: Scarf

Crocheting is an activity that can be both therapeutic and practical. It's a relaxing pastime that allows you to create unique and personalized pieces. One of the most popular and straightforward crochet projects for beginners is the scarf. It is simple to make, and you have the chance to experiment with different shapes, styles, and patterns.

Crocheting a scarf is the ideal project for anyone new to the world of crochet. It is the perfect first project because it doesn't require any complicated patterns or techniques. You can practice basic stitches, such as the chain, single crochet, and double crochet, while working on the scarf. Once you learn these foundational stitches, you can move on to more complex crocheting projects.

Before you start your crochet project, you need to choose your yarn and hook. The weight of the yarn determines the size of your hook. Depending on the thickness of the yarn, you'll need to use a hook that complements it. For example, if you're using a lightweight yarn, you'll need to use a smaller hook. On the other hand, if you're using a bulky yarn, you'll need to use a larger hook. Once you have chosen your yarn and hook, it's time to start crocheting.

If you're new to crocheting, it's essential to start with a simple pattern and stick to it until you feel comfortable with the stitches. One of the most basic patterns you can use for a scarf is the single crochet stitch. The single crochet stitch is easy to learn and creates a dense and sturdy fabric. To start, make a slipknot, and then chain the desired length of your scarf. Once you've chained your desired length of the scarf, you can start your single crochet stitch.

To start your single crochet stitch, insert your hook through the second chain from the hook. Wrap your yarn around the hook, and pull it back through the chain. You should have two loops on your hook. Wrap your yarn around the hook again, and draw it through both loops on your hook. Continue this process until you reach the end of your chain. When you reach the end of your chain, turn your work and start a new row. Repeat this process until your scarf is the desired length.

Once you've learned how to single crochet, you can experiment with other patterns and stitches. The double crochet stitch is a popular stitch for scarfs. It's a little bit trickier than the single crochet stitch, but once you get the hang of it, it's easy to do. To do the double crochet stitch, wrap your yarn around your hook, insert your hook into the stitch or space you're working in, then pull the yarn through the stitch or space. You should have three loops on your hook. Wrap the yarn around the hook again and draw it through the first two loops on the hook. Wrap the yarn around the hook once more and draw it through the remaining two loops.

The half double crochet stitch is another popular stitch for scarfs. It's a stitch that falls in between the single crochet and double crochet stitches in terms of length. To do the half double crochet stitch, wrap your yarn around your hook, insert your hook into the stitch or space you're working in, then pull the yarn through the stitch or space. You should have three loops on your hook. Wrap the yarn around the hook again and draw it through all three loops on your hook.

Once you've mastered basic stitches, you can start trying out different patterns for your scarf. Some patterns involve using multiple colors, while others incorporate different textures and stitch patterns. Patterns like the shell stitch or the ripple stitch are good options for creating a more textured look for your scarf.

In addition to experimenting with different patterns, you can also customize your scarf with different embellishments. One popular embellishment for scarfs is tassels. To add tassels to your scarf, cut lengths of yarn twice the length you want your tassels to be. Fold the lengths of yarn in half and use your crochet hook to draw the looped end through the edge of the scarf. Then, thread the loose ends of the yarn through the loop and pull tight. Repeat this process until you have the desired number of tassels.
Crocheting a scarf is a simple and rewarding project that's perfect for beginners. It's an excellent way to learn basic stitches while creating a practical and fashionable item. With endless possibilities for customization and personalization, you can create a scarf that's unique to you. So grab some yarn and a hook, and start crocheting your own scarf today!

Chapter 22: Crochet Project: Beanie Hat

Crochet is an art form that has been practiced for centuries. It is a form of needlework that involves using a hook and yarn to create beautiful and intricate designs. The art of crochet is popular all over the world, and it has been passed down from generation to generation. It is a relaxing and therapeutic form of art that can provide hours of enjoyment.

The art of crochet has many benefits. It can help with hand-eye coordination and fine motor skills, making it an excellent activity for children and the elderly. It is also a great way to relieve stress and anxiety, providing a sense of accomplishment and relaxation upon the completion of a project.

There are countless types of projects that can be created through crochet, from intricate afghans to simple scarves. One of the most popular projects for beginners is the beanie hat. In this chapter, we will explore the process of creating a beanie hat through crochet.

Choosing the Right Yarn and Hook

Before beginning any crochet project, it is important to choose the right yarn and hook. For a beanie hat, a medium weight yarn is recommended, as it is easy to work with and provides a good balance of warmth and durability. The hook size will depend on the thickness of the yarn and the size of the hat being created.

When selecting yarn, it is important to consider the color and texture of the yarn. Neutral colors such as black, gray, and beige are versatile and can be worn with many different outfits. Bright colors such as pink, purple, and blue can add a pop of color to a winter outfit.

Creating a Magic Circle

The first step in creating a beanie hat is creating a magic circle. This technique is used to create a tight center that will prevent any holes from forming when starting the first round.

To create a magic circle, start by holding the tail of the yarn between your thumb and forefinger. Use your other hand to wrap the yarn around your index and middle fingers twice, forming a loop around your fingers. Insert the hook into the circle and catch the yarn with the hook. Pull the yarn through the center of the loop and chain one, securing the loop.

Working the First Round

Once the magic circle has been created, it is time to start the first round. This will be the base of the beanie hat.

To start the first round, chain two. Then, work twelve double crochets into the center of the magic circle. To create a double crochet, yarn over, insert the hook into the center of the circle, yarn over again, and pull through. Yarn over once more and pull through two loops on the hook. Yarn over again and pull through the remaining two loops.

Once all twelve double crochets have been completed, slip stitch into the top of the first double crochet, joining the round.

Working the Second Round

To begin the second round, chain two and work two double crochets into each stitch around the circle. This will create a total of 24 stitches. Slip stitch into the top of the first double crochet, joining the round.

Working the Third Round

To start the third round, chain two and work one double crochet into the next stitch. Work two double crochets into the next stitch and continue alternating between one and two double crochets in each stitch around the circle. Slip stitch into the top of the first double crochet, joining the round.

Working the Fourth Round

For the fourth round, chain two and work one double crochet into each stitch around the circle. Slip stitch into the top of the first double crochet, joining the round.

Working the Fifth Round

The fifth round is where the beanie hat begins to take shape. To start, chain two and work one double crochet into the first stitch. Work one double crochet into each of the next two stitches. Then, work two double crochets into the next stitch. Repeat this pattern around the circle. Slip stitch into the top of the first double crochet, joining the round.

Working the Sixth through Ninth Rounds

For rounds six through nine, continue to alternate between one and two double crochets in each stitch around the circle, with an additional stitch added to each section. In round six, work one double crochet into the first stitch, then one double crochet into each of the next three stitches, followed by two double crochets in the next stitch. This pattern will continue through round nine.

Working the Tenth Round

For the tenth round, work one double crochet into each stitch around the circle. Slip stitch into the top of the first double crochet, joining the round.

Working the Eleventh Round

The eleventh round is where the beanie hat will be shaped to fit the head. To start the eleventh round, chain one and work one single crochet into the first stitch. Work one single crochet into each of the next five stitches. Then, work two single crochets together over the next two stitches. Repeat this pattern around the circle. Slip stitch into the top of the first single crochet, joining the round.

Working the Twelfth Round

For the twelfth round, work one single crochet into each stitch around the circle. Slip stitch into the top of the first single crochet, joining the round.

Finishing the Beanie Hat

To finish the beanie hat, fasten off the yarn and weave in any loose ends. The beanie hat can be worn as is, or embellished with pom-poms or buttons.

Creating a beanie hat through crochet is a great introduction to the art of crochet. It is a simple project that can be completed in a short amount of time, providing a sense of accomplishment. By following the steps outlined in this chapter, anyone can create a beautiful and functional beanie hat to keep themselves or a loved one warm during the winter months.

Chapter 23: Crochet Project: Dishcloth

Crochet is a popular hobby that allows people to create beautiful and functional items. One such project is the dishcloth. This small and practical item is perfect for beginners who want to learn how to crochet. It is also a great way to use up leftover yarn and reduce waste. In this chapter, we will explore how to crochet a dishcloth and the different patterns you can try.

Materials Needed

To make a dishcloth, you will need a few basic materials. These include:

1. Yarn – choose a soft and absorbent yarn that can withstand frequent use and cleaning. Cotton and bamboo yarns are excellent choices for dishcloths.

2. Crochet hook – select a hook size that matches the thickness of your yarn. The most common hook sizes for dishcloths include 4.5mm, 5mm, and 5.5mm.

3. Scissors – you will need scissors to cut your yarn and trim any loose ends.

4. Tapestry needle – a tapestry needle is ideal for weaving in ends and sewing pieces together.

Crochet Stitches for Dishcloths

There are several crochet stitches you can use to create different textures and patterns in your dishcloths. The most common crochet stitches for dishcloths include:

1. Single Crochet (SC) – this is one of the easiest stitches to learn and is perfect for beginners. It creates a dense and sturdy fabric that is ideal for dishcloths.

2. Half-Double Crochet (HDC) – this stitch is slightly taller than the SC stitch and creates a textured fabric that is perfect for scrubbing.

3. Double Crochet (DC) – this stitch is taller than the HDC stitch and creates a looser and lighter fabric that is ideal for delicate dishware.

4. Treble Crochet (TR) – this stitch is the tallest crochet stitch and creates a lacy and airy fabric that is perfect for decorative dishcloths.

Crochet Pattern for a Simple Dishcloth

Now that you have your materials and stitches in mind, let's get started on a simple dishcloth pattern that uses the single crochet stitch.

Step 1: Make a slip knot and chain 25 stitches.

Step 2: Starting from the second chain from the hook, SC in each stitch until the end of the row.

Step 3: Chain 1, turn your work, and SC in each stitch until the end of the row.

Step 4: Repeat step 3 until your dishcloth measures approximately 8 inches in length.

Step 5: Cut your yarn and weave in the ends using a tapestry needle.

Congratulations, you have just completed your first dishcloth!

Crochet Pattern for a Textured Dishcloth

If you want to add more texture to your dishcloth, you can try the half-double crochet stitch. This pattern will create a ridged fabric that is perfect for scrubbing.

Step 1: Make a slip knot and chain 25 stitches.

Step 2: Starting from the second chain from the hook, HDC in each stitch until the end of the row.

Step 3: Chain 1, turn your work, and HDC in the back loop of each stitch until the end of the row. This creates a ridge effect.

Step 4: Repeat step 3 until your dishcloth measures approximately 8 inches in length.

Step 5: Cut your yarn and weave in the ends using a tapestry needle.

Crochet Pattern for a Diagonal Dishcloth

If you want to try something more challenging, you can try crocheting a diagonal dishcloth. This pattern uses the double crochet stitch and creates a unique diamond shape.

Step 1: Make a slip knot and chain 26 stitches.

Step 2: Starting from the third chain from the hook, DC in each stitch until the end of the row.

Step 3: Chain 2, turn your work, and DC in each stitch until the second last stitch.

Step 4: DC2tog (double crochet two together) in the last two stitches.

Step 5: Chain 2, turn your work, DC in each stitch until the second last stitch.

Step 6: DC2tog in the last two stitches.

Step 7: Repeat steps 5-6 until you have 3 stitches left.

Step 8: DC in the last 3 stitches.

Step 9: Turn your work and DC in each stitch across.

Step 10: Repeat steps 2-9 until your dishcloth reaches the desired size.

Step 11: Cut your yarn and weave in the ends using a tapestry needle.

Crocheting a dishcloth is a fun and rewarding project that allows you to practice your crochet skills while creating a useful item. You can experiment with different stitches, patterns, and colors to create unique and personalized dishcloths for yourself or as gifts. Whether you are a beginner or an experienced crocheter, there is a dishcloth pattern that is perfect for you. So why not grab your yarn and hook and get started on your next crochet project today?

Chapter 24: Crochet Project: Granny Square

Crochet is a versatile craft that has been practiced for centuries, producing a variety of beautiful and functional items such as blankets, clothing, and home decor. Granny squares are one of the most popular and well-known crochet motifs, and they have been used in countless projects over the years. In this chapter, we will delve into the history of crochet and the granny square, explore the different styles and techniques involved in making them, and discuss some project ideas to get you started.

The History of Crochet

The origins of crochet are somewhat shrouded in mystery, as the craft seems to have evolved gradually over time rather than being invented by one person or culture. Some historians believe that crochet may have developed from earlier forms of needlework such as tambour embroidery or Irish lace-making, while others speculate that it may have been influenced by traditional Tunisian or Egyptian weaving techniques. Regardless of its precise origins, crochet has a rich history that spans continents and cultures, from the lace-making traditions of Europe to the colorful tapestries of South America and beyond.

In the early days of crochet, the craft was primarily used to make lace and fine garments for wealthy patrons. Crochet hooks were often made of expensive materials such as ivory or tortoiseshell, and intricate patterns were worked with delicate thread or silk. As the craft grew in popularity throughout the 19th century, however, it began to shift towards more practical applications such as household items and clothing for the middle and working classes.

The Granny Square

One of the most iconic and enduring designs in crochet is the granny square. This simple, square motif is made up of clusters of double crochet stitches and is typically worked in multiple colors to create a bold and vibrant design. Although the exact origins of the granny square are unclear, it is thought to have become popular in the 1960s and 1970s as part of the hippie fashion movement. Since then, the granny square has remained a staple in the crochet world and has been used in a variety of projects ranging from blankets and pillows to clothing and accessories.

Granny Squares: Types and Techniques

There are many different styles and techniques involved in making granny squares, each with its own unique look and feel. Some of the most common types of granny squares include:

Traditional Granny Square

The traditional granny square is made up of a basic cluster stitch pattern that creates a solid central square surrounded by a border of chain stitches. This style of granny square is fairly simple to learn and is great for beginner crocheters.

Solid Granny Square

The solid granny square is similar to the traditional granny square but is worked entirely in double crochet stitches, giving it a more uniform and solid appearance.

Granny Square with a Circle Center

This type of granny square features a circular center made up of a spiral of single crochet stitches, which is then surrounded by a more traditional granny square pattern.

Granny Square with a Flower Center

Another variation on the classic granny square, this style features a small floral motif in the center of the square. This can be achieved by working a series of slip stitches and single crochets to create the petals of the flower.

Granny Square with a Popcorn Center

This style of granny square features a popcorn stitch in the center of the square, giving it a raised and textured appearance. Popcorn stitches are created by working a set number of double crochets into the same stitch and then pulling the loop through them all at once.

Once you have chosen a style of granny square to work with, there are several different techniques that you can use to give your squares different textures and effects. Some of these techniques include:

Color Changing

One of the key features of a granny square is the use of multiple colors to create a bold and eye-catching pattern. To change colors, you simply work up to the last two loops of the final double crochet stitch in your current color, then drop the old color and pull through the new color to complete the stitch. You can then continue working with the new color for the rest of the row.

Striped Granny Squares

To create a striped effect in your granny square, you can alternate rows of different colors or work them in a specific pattern. This can give your squares a more orderly and structured appearance.

Random Color Mixing

If you prefer a more organic and spontaneous look, you can mix colors at random as you work your granny squares. This can lead to some surprising and delightful color combinations!

Joining Granny Squares

Once you have created a number of granny squares, you will need to join them together to form your final project. There are a few different methods for joining granny squares, including whip stitching, slip stitching, and crochet join-as-you-go techniques.

Whip Stitching

Whip stitching involves sewing your granny squares together with a needle and thread. To do this, you simply lay two squares side by side and sew through the back loops of the stitches on each side.

Slip Stitching

Slip stitching involves working an additional row of slip stitches around the edge of each square, then crocheting them together with a slip stitch join. This can give your finished project a more polished and professional look.

Crochet Join-as-you-go

This technique involves working your granny squares together as you go, crocheting them directly to each other rather than joining them separately. This can be a bit more complicated than the other techniques but can lead to a more seamless and cohesive final product.

Project Ideas

Now that we have explored the different types and techniques involved in making granny squares, let's take a look at some project ideas to inspire you:

Granny Square Blanket

A classic use for granny squares is to create a cozy, colorful blanket. You can choose a specific color scheme or mix and match at random to create a whimsical and unique design. You can also experiment with different joining techniques to give your blanket a distinctive look.

Granny Square Scarf

A granny square scarf is a fun and playful accessory that can keep you warm in style. You can use different patterns and colors to create a one-of-a-kind design, and you can adjust the size of your squares to create a more delicate or chunky scarf as desired.

Granny Square Pillow

A granny square pillow can add a pop of color and texture to any room. You can create a single large square for the front of your pillow and join several smaller squares for the back, or you can create a full cover with a series of larger squares joined together.

Granny Square Bag

A granny square bag is a simple and stylish accessory that can be customized in countless ways. You can use a variety of colors and patterns and experiment with different shapes and sizes to create a bag that is uniquely yours.

In this chapter, we have explored the history of crochet and the granny square, delved into the different styles and techniques involved in making them, and discussed some project ideas to get you started. Whether you are a seasoned crocheter or just starting out, the granny square is a versatile and endlessly creative motif that can be used in a variety of projects. So grab your hook and some colorful yarn and let your imagination run wild!

Chapter 25: Crochet Project: Baby Booties

If you are looking for a crochet project that is both fun and practical, then why not make a pair of baby booties? They are a perfect gift for a new parent or a wonderful addition to your own baby's wardrobe. The great thing about baby booties is that they come in a variety of designs and styles, from basic to whimsical. You can choose to make them in simple, neutral colors or go all out with bright and bold hues.

In this chapter, we will introduce you to the world of crochet baby booties, including the materials you will need, the basic techniques you should know, and tips and tricks to make your project a success. So, gather your yarn, hook, and other supplies, and let's get started!

Materials and Tools

Before you begin your crochet project, you need to make sure you have all the necessary materials and tools. Here is a list of what you will need to make baby booties:

- Yarn: Choose a soft, washable yarn that is appropriate for baby items. Some popular brands that make baby-friendly yarns are Bernat, Caron, and Red Heart.

- Crochet Hook: The size of your hook will depend on the size of the baby booties you want to make. Generally, a size G (4.25mm) or H (5mm) hook is used for most patterns.

- Stitch Markers: These are helpful for keeping track of where you are in your project. They can be either locking or removable.

- Scissors: You will need a pair of sharp scissors to cut the yarn when you finish your project.

- Tapestry Needle: This is used for weaving in the loose ends of yarn.

- Button or Ribbon: Optional embellishments that can be used to add a decorative touch.

Basic Techniques

If you are new to crochet, don't worry. Baby booties are a great project for beginners because they are small and easy to work with. Here are some basic techniques you should know before you start your project:

- Chain Stitch: This is the foundation of most crochet projects. To make a chain stitch, loop the yarn over the hook and pull it through the loop on the hook. Continue this process until you have the desired number of stitches.

- Single Crochet: This is the most basic stitch. To make a single crochet, insert the hook into the next stitch, yarn over the hook, and pull the yarn through the stitch. Yarn over again and pull through both loops on the hook.

- Double Crochet: This stitch is taller than the single crochet. To make a double crochet, yarn over the hook, insert the hook into the next stitch, yarn over again, and pull the yarn through the stitch. Yarn over again and pull through two loops on the hook, then yarn over one more time and pull through the last two loops.

- Slip Stitch: This stitch is used to join the end of a round to the beginning. To make a slip stitch, insert the hook into the next stitch, yarn over the hook, and pull the yarn through both the stitch and the loop on the hook.

Patterns

Now that you know the basic techniques, it's time to choose a pattern. There are many free patterns available online, but here are three of our favorite baby bootie patterns:

- Basic Baby Booties: This pattern is perfect for beginners. It uses only single crochet stitches and is worked in rounds. The booties are customizable based on the size you want to make.
- Mary Jane Baby Booties: These booties are sweet and feminine, with a strap that fastens across the top. They are worked in rounds and involve several different stitches, such as double crochet, slip stitch, and chain stitch.
- Animal Baby Booties: These adorable booties come in a variety of animal designs, such as pandas, lions, and elephants. The patterns are a bit more challenging than the previous two, but the end result

is worth it! They use a combination of single crochet, double crochet, and slip stitch.

Tips and Tricks

Here are some tips and tricks to keep in mind when making baby booties:

- Gauge: Make sure you follow the gauge listed in the pattern. This will ensure that your finished product is the correct size.
- Yarn Selection: Choose a soft, washable yarn that is appropriate for baby items. Avoid yarns that have any scratchy textures or fibers that might aggravate sensitive skin.
- Stitch Markers: Use stitch markers to keep track of where you are in your pattern. This can help prevent mistakes and make it easier to count your stitches.
- Crochet in Good Lighting: Crochet in a well-lit area to avoid strain on your eyes.
- Practice: If you are new to crochet, practice the basic stitches before starting your project. This will improve your speed and accuracy.

Making baby booties is a fun and rewarding crochet project. Whether you are making them for your own little one or as a gift, they are sure to be cherished for years to come. With a few basic supplies, some practice, and a little bit of patience, you can create a beautiful and functional set of booties that any baby will love.

Chapter 26: Introduction to Crochet in the Round

Crocheting is a craft that has been practiced by people all over the world for centuries. It is a versatile form of creating textile-based items by using yarn, thread, and a crochet hook. Crocheting can involve working in rows, but it is often preferred to crochet in a continuous circle or round. Crocheting in the round is the technique of creating crochet projects that are circular or tubular in shape. It can be used to create hats, bags, stuffed animals, and many other items.

This chapter will introduce you to crocheting in the round. We will discuss the basics of working in a circular pattern, how to increase and decrease stitches, and the different types of stitches that can be used. By the end of this chapter, you will be able to create your own circular projects with confidence.

Getting Started

Before you start crocheting in the round, you will need a few basic supplies. You will need a crochet hook, yarn, and a stitch marker. It is also a good idea to have a crochet pattern or a design in mind before starting. Choose a pattern that is appropriate for your experience level, and make sure it specifies that the project is worked in the round.

When working in the round, it is essential to use a stitch marker to keep track of the beginning of the round. You can use a safety pin, a piece of contrasting yarn, or a specialized stitch marker designed for crocheting. Place the marker in the first stitch of the round and move it up to each new round as you work.

Starting a Round

To start a round, you will need to make a slipknot and chain a certain number of stitches, depending on the pattern. Some patterns may require you to join the chain into a ring by slant stitching the first stitch to the last. Others may require you to work directly into the first chain stitch to create a continuous circle. Once you have joined your stitches, be sure to place a stitch marker in the first stitch. This will be your starting point for the next round.

A common method of starting a round when working in the round is the magic ring, also known as magic circle or magic loop. The magic ring is a technique used to create a closed loop with a small hole in the center, which is perfect for creating circular projects.

To create a magic ring, wrap the yarn around your fingers with the tail in the back and the working yarn in the front. Take the hook and insert it under the first piece of yarn. Pull the yarn through, leaving a loop on your hook. Chain one to secure the loop.

Insert the hook into the center of the loop and pull up a loop of yarn. This loop will serve as your first stitch. Work the required number of stitches into the loop, and pull the tail to close the loop. Be sure to place a stitch marker in the first stitch.

Once you have joined your stitches or created a magic ring, you are ready to start working in the round.

Working in the Round

When working in the round, you will be creating a spiral pattern. Unlike working in rows, there is no turning at the end of each row. When you reach the end of the round, you simply continue to work in the same direction, following the spiral.

To work in the round, you will insert the hook into the top of the first stitch, yarn over, and pull up a loop. You will then repeat this process into each stitch around. Be sure to work around the stitch marker and not to include it in your stitches.

There are two main methods of crocheting in the round – using the single crochet stitch and the double crochet stitch.

Single Crochet in the Round

The single crochet is the most basic stitch used when crocheting in the round. It creates a dense, sturdy fabric that is perfect for items like amigurumi and hats. To work in single crochet in the round, you will insert your hook into the top of the first stitch, yarn over, and pull up a loop. You will then yarn over again and pull through both loops on the hook.

To continue working in the round, you will insert your hook into the top of the next stitch, yarn over, and repeat the process.

Double Crochet in the Round

The double crochet stitch is a taller, looser stitch that creates a more open and drapey fabric. It is commonly used when creating items like shawls or blankets. To work in double crochet in the round, you will yarn over, then insert your hook into the top of the first stitch. Yarn over again and pull up a loop. You will then yarn over and pull through two loops on the hook. Repeat this process until you have worked into each stitch in the round.

Increasing and Decreasing Stitches

To create a circular project that increases in size, you will need to increase the number of stitches in each round. This can be done by working two or more stitches into the same stitch. To increase in single crochet stitch, work two single crochets into the next stitch. To increase in double crochet stitch, work two double crochets into the next stitch.

To decrease the number of stitches in a round, you will need to work two or more stitches together. This can be done by inserting the hook into two or more stitches and working a single stitch, decreasing the number of stitches. To decrease in single crochet stitch, insert your hook into the next stitch and pull up a loop. Insert your hook into the following stitch and pull up another loop. Yarn over and pull through all three loops on the hook. To decrease in double crochet stitch, insert your hook into the next stitch and yarn over. Insert your hook into the following stitch and pull up a loop. Yarn over and pull through the first two loops on the hook. Yarn over again and pull through the last two loops on the hook.

Crocheting in the round is a versatile and fun technique that can be used to create a wide range of projects. By following the tips and techniques outlined in this chapter, you can confidently create your own circular projects with ease. Remember to use a stitch marker to keep track of your rounds, and to practice increasing and decreasing stitches to achieve your desired result. With practice and patience, you can become skilled at crocheting in the round, and take your crochet skills to the next level.

Chapter 27: Learning the Magic Ring Technique

As a crochet enthusiast, I've always been fascinated with the magic ring technique. It's a magical and ingenious way of starting a project and creating a seamless circle. The technique is especially useful for creating projects such as amigurumi, hats, and mandalas among others. If you've never learned the magic ring technique, don't fret, in this chapter, we'll explore the ins and outs of this crochet technique.

Before delving deeper into the technique, let's first address the elephant in the room - the slip knot. The slip knot is used to start most crochet projects, and if you're new to crocheting, you've probably used it before. However, the magic ring technique replaces the slip knot with a circular ring. With a slip knot, you're limited to creating an opening that's often too small or too big, and can leave an unsightly hole in the center of your work. The magic ring is an alternative to the slip knot, and it allows you to create a custom-sized and seamless ring that's perfect for starting most crochet projects.

Learning the Magic Ring Technique

Step One: Hold your yarn.

Start by holding your yarn and creating a loop with your non-dominant hand. The loop should be big enough to fit your fingers inside but not too big that it's unwieldy. Position the loose end of your yarn over the loop, making sure that it rests underneath the working yarn.

Step Two: Create a ring.

Using your crochet hook, insert it from the front into the loop - so that the hook is underneath the yarn tail. Grab hold of the working yarn - the yarn attached to your skein, and pull it through the loop with your hook.

Step Three: Chain.

Create a chain stitch using the hook and the working yarn. This chain stitch will serve as the first stitch of your project.

Step Four: Stitch.

Create your first round of stitches inside the ring, using the hook and the working yarn. The number of stitches you need will vary depending on the pattern you're following. Work your stitches around the loop, retaining the tension and making sure the stitches are tightly tugged to form a ring.

Step Five: Close the ring.

Once you've completed your stitches around the ring, you'll need to close it. To do so, grab hold of the free end of your yarn with your fingers and gently pull it, tightening the loop in the center of the ring until it's almost closed. Using your crochet hook, slip stitch through the first stitch you made in the circle to complete the ring.

Step Six: Weave in loose ends.

Now that you've finished your magic ring, you'll need to weave in your loose ends. Insert the hook onto the back of your project and weave the loose yarn ends through the existing stitches. Continue until you've weaved in all the loose yarn ends.

Tips and Tricks For Learning the Magic Ring Technique

- Practice, practice, practice! Like any skill in crocheting, learning the magic ring technique requires patience, and it's possible you may not get it right the first time. Keep practicing until you've mastered the technique.
- Keep your stitches tight. Tight stitches prevent holes and a lop-sided ring.
- Use the right yarn weight. Yarn thickness can impact the success of your magic ring. If your yarn is too thick, it might be too difficult to create small tight stitches. If the yarn weight is too light, the ring may not hold its shape.
- Watch tutorials. Sometimes, it's easier to understand a technique when you see it in action. You can find many videos on YouTube that demonstrate the magic ring technique.
- Select the appropriate hook size. The size of your crochet hook determines the size of your project as well as the hook's tension.

Using a hook that's too small or too big can affect the success of your projects.

- Always practice safety. Be careful when using crochet hooks as they have pointed ends that can hurt.

The magic ring technique is a unique way of starting your crochet projects that can elevate the look of your final product. It's important to master the technique so that you can start your projects effortlessly and ensure a neat finish. With the right materials, practice, and patience, you'll have no trouble learning the magic ring technique, and soon it will be a part of your set of crochet skills. Happy crocheting!

Chapter 28: Understanding Color Changes in Crochet

Crochet is a technique that involves using yarn or thread to create various patterns and designs by interlocking loops. One of the essential aspects of crochet is color, which adds life and personality to the finished piece. Understanding how to incorporate color into crochet can elevate your projects from drab to fab.

In this chapter, we'll explore color changes in crochet. We'll look at the different techniques to change colors, how to avoid color pooling, and how to read color charts. We'll also discuss color theory and color psychology, which are crucial in determining the right color combinations for your crochet projects.

The Different Techniques for Changing Colors

There are different techniques for changing colors in crochet. The most basic method is the cut and tie method, where you cut the old color and tie the new color to the old yarn's tail. Although this method is the easiest to execute, it uses a lot of yarn and creates an excess of yarn tails that you'll have to weave in later on.

Another technique is the invisible join method, which involves crocheting to the end of the row with the old color, then joining the new color with a slip stitch. This method creates a seamless transition between colors, but it can be tricky to execute, especially for beginners.

The most common technique for changing colors is the yarn over (YO) method. This method involves wrapping the new color over the old color and pulling the new color through the last two loops of the old color. It's less bulky than the cut and tie method and doesn't require additional weaving in of yarn tails. However, it creates a small gap between the colors, which can be noticeable in some projects.

Avoiding Color Pooling

Color pooling is an unintentional color pattern that can occur when you change colors. It happens when the colors stack or pool on top of each other, creating a blotchy or uneven effect. Color pooling is generally undesirable, especially when working with variegated yarns that have a unique color pattern.

The key to avoiding color pooling is to understand your yarn's color repeats and match your stitch count to that pattern. You can do this by counting the number of stitches it takes for the colors to repeat, then adjusting your stitches to match that count.

Another way to avoid color pooling is to use a larger or smaller hook than recommended by the yarn's label. This will affect the gauge, which can change the way the colors stack. Using a larger hook creates wider stitches, which can blend the colors better, while using a smaller hook creates tighter stitches that can create a striped effect.

Reading Color Charts

Color charts are essential when working on color-intensive crochet projects, such as granny squares, mandalas, or afghans. A color chart is a visual representation of your project with different colors represented by symbols.

The most common type of color chart is the color block chart, where each block represents a stitch in the pattern. You can also use a symbol chart, where each symbol represents a stitch. Both types of charts can be printed or digital, which makes them easier to read and follow.

To read a color chart, you need to start at the bottom right corner and work your way up to the left. Each row is read from right to left or left to right, depending on the pattern. The symbols or colors in each row represent the stitches you need to make for that row.

Understanding Color Theory and Color Psychology

Understanding color theory and color psychology is crucial in determining the right color combinations for your crochet projects. Color theory is the science of color, where colors are classified based on their properties and attributes. Color psychology is the study of how colors affect human behavior and emotions.

Color theory is based on the color wheel, which is a visual

representation of the primary, secondary, and tertiary colors. The primary colors are red, blue, and yellow, which cannot be created by mixing other colors. Secondary colors are purple, green, and orange, which are created by mixing two primary colors. Tertiary colors are created by mixing a primary and a secondary color.

Color psychology is based on the emotional associations that people have with different colors. For example, red is associated with love, passion, and anger, while blue is associated with calmness, trust, and loyalty. The emotional associations can vary depending on the culture, context, and personal experiences.

When choosing colors for your crochet project, you need to consider both color theory and color psychology. You need to determine if the colors complement each other based on their properties, and if they convey the right emotions and message based on color psychology.

Color changes in crochet are essential in creating eye-catching and beautiful projects. The right color combination can elevate a simple pattern, while the wrong color combination can ruin a complex pattern. Understanding the different techniques for changing colors, avoiding color pooling, and reading color charts can make your crochet projects look more polished and professional.

Color theory and color psychology are the foundation of color selection in crochet. By understanding the properties and emotional associations of different colors, you can create projects that reflect your personality and intentions. Remember to have fun and experiment with different color combinations. The beauty of crochet is that you can always undo your stitches and try again.

Chapter 29: Learning Tapestry Crochet

Tapestry crochet is a popular crochet technique that allows you to create a stunning tapestry design on your crochet project. This technique involves using multiple strands of yarn at the same time to create a dense fabric with beautiful designs. Unlike regular crochet, where only one strand of yarn is used, tapestry crochet requires more yarn and is worked in a specific way to create a design. Tapestry crochet can be done in a variety of patterns, shapes, and colors, giving you endless possibilities for your crochet projects!

Learning tapestry crochet can seem intimidating at first, but with the right tools, tips, and techniques, anyone can master this unique crocheting style. In this chapter, we will explore the basics of tapestry crochet, including materials needed, stitches used, and a step-by-step guide to creating your first tapestry crochet project.

Materials Needed

The first step to learning tapestry crochet is to gather the necessary materials. Here are some materials that you'll need when learning to do tapestry crochet:

Yarn - Tapestry crochet uses multiple strands of yarn at the same time. You can use two, three, or even four strands of yarn, depending on your design and desired effect. When choosing yarn, ensure that they have the same weight so that each strand will have equal tension.

Crochet Hook - You'll need a crochet hook that suits your yarn. A hook with a soft, comfortable grip is also recommended. It's best to use a hook that is about one size larger than you would normally use for your yarn. For example, if your yarn recommends a 5mm crochet hook, use a 6mm hook instead.

Tapestry Crochet Pattern - A tapestry crochet pattern will help guide you in creating your design. You can find these patterns online, in books, or create your own.

Scissors - A good pair of scissors is essential for cutting your yarn.

Tapestry Needle - A tapestry needle is great for weaving in your ends. You'll want one that's suitable for the weight of your yarn.

Stitches Used

While tapestry crochet uses a variety of stitches, there are two main stitches you'll need to know:

Single Crochet (SC) - The single crochet stitch is the most basic stitch in crochet. To do a single crochet stitch, insert your hook into the stitch, yarn over, and pull up a loop. Then, yarn over again and pull through both loops on your hook.

Color Change - Changing colors in tapestry crochet is critical to creating patterns and designs. To do this, work your last single crochet stitch of the row up to the final two loops on your hook. Drop your current color and pick up your new color. Then, yarn over with the new color and pull it through the final two loops of your single crochet stitch.

Basic Steps to Creating a Project

Now that you know what materials you'll need and the basic stitches in tapestry crochet, it's time to start creating your project. Here's a step-by-step guide to get you started:

Step 1: Choose Your Design - Choose a design you want to create. Keep in mind that simple designs are best for beginners as they involve only a few color changes.

Step 2: Choose Your Yarn - Select the colors you want to use to create your design.

Step 3: Create a Foundation Chain - Create a foundation chain in the length that you want. The foundation chain will act as the base for the entire project. If you're not sure how long to make it, measure your finished item and make the foundation chain a little bit longer.

Step 4: Join Your Yarn - Join your first color of yarn to your hook and insert your hook into the first stitch of the foundation chain.

Step 5: Start Crocheting - Work the first row of single crochet stitches. Crochet according to your pattern and change the color as necessary to create your design.

Step 6: Repeat - Repeat Step 5 until you have completed the desired number of rows.

Step 7: Finish - Once you have completed your pattern, fasten off your yarn and weave in the ends.

Tips and Tricks

Now that you know the basics of tapestry crochet, here are some tips and tricks that can help you create an even better tapestry crochet project:

1. Keep your yarn organized - Tapestry crochet requires using multiple strands of yarn at the same time. To keep your yarn organized, you can use bobbins or clothespins to prevent tangling.

2. Keep your tension consistent - Consistent tension is essential in tapestry crochet to achieve an even result. Be sure to keep an even tension throughout the project.

3. Practice makes perfect - Tapestry crochet can be intimidating for beginners, but with practice, you'll get more comfortable with the technique. Take your time, and don't be afraid to rip out stitches if

necessary.

4. Use graph paper - If you're creating your own tapestry crochet pattern, use graph paper to plan and create your design.

5. Joining rounds - To make your crochet project look seamless, learn how to join rounds without any visible join or seam.

Tapestry crochet is a beautiful technique that can add a unique touch to any crochet project. By learning the basic materials, stitches, and techniques used in tapestry crochet, you'll be on your way to creating beautiful and intricate designs in your crochet projects. Remember to take your time, practice, and have fun with your projects - the possibilities are endless!

Chapter 30: Learning Filet Crochet

Filet crochet is a beautiful and versatile type of crochet that is based on a grid pattern. It is named after "filet," which is the French word for "net," as this type of crochet creates a mesh-like fabric that is perfect for creating intricate designs and patterns. If you are interested in learning filet crochet, this guide will walk you through the basic techniques and tips you need to get started.

Materials and Tools

Before you can start filet crochet, you will need to gather a few basic materials and tools. The most important item you will need is a crochet hook. The size of the crochet hook you use will depend on the thickness of the yarn you choose. For beginners, it is recommended to use a size G or H hook with worsted weight yarn.

You will also need to choose your yarn. Filet crochet works well with any type of yarn, from lightweight cotton to bulky wool. However, when starting out, it is best to choose a smooth, medium-weight yarn that is easy to see your stitches in. Light colors also tend to work better, as they make it easier to see the intricate designs you will be creating.

Finally, you will need a pattern to follow. There are many free filet crochet patterns available online, or you can create your own by working from graph paper. When choosing a pattern, it is important to make sure it is the right size for your project. You can adjust the size of the pattern by changing the number of stitches you cast on.

Basic Techniques

Now that you have your materials and tools ready, it is time to start crocheting! The first thing you need to do is cast on. To do this, make a slip knot in your yarn and then insert your crochet hook into the knot. Yarn over and pull the loop through the knot, creating a new loop on your hook. Continue this process until you have the required number of stitches for your pattern.

Once you have cast on, you are ready to start crocheting your first row. For filet crochet, there are two types of stitches you can use: the double crochet (dc) and the chain stitch (ch). The double crochet stitch is the most common and is used to create the solid blocks in your pattern. The chain stitch is used to create the empty spaces in your pattern.

To work a double crochet stitch, yarn over your hook and insert it into the next stitch. Yarn over again and pull the loop through the stitch, leaving three loops on your hook. Yarn over again and pull the loop through the first two loops on your hook, leaving two loops. Yarn over again and pull the loop through the last two loops on your hook, completing the stitch.

To work a chain stitch, yarn over and pull through the loop on your hook. This will create a new loop, which you can then use to begin your next stitch.

As you work your first row, you will need to pay attention to the pattern you are following. This will tell you when to work double crochet stitches and when to work chain stitches. If you are working with a graph paper pattern, you can use a highlighter or marker to mark the stitches you need to work.

After you have finished your first row, you will need to turn your work and begin working on the next row. In filet crochet, you will always work on the right side of your fabric, so you will need to turn your work after each row to keep the right side facing you.

As you work your rows, you will start to see the pattern taking shape. The solid blocks will create the design, while the empty spaces will form the background. It is important to pay close attention to your pattern as you work, as this will help ensure your design is accurate and consistent.

Advanced Techniques

Once you have mastered the basic techniques of filet crochet, you can start to experiment with more advanced techniques and stitches. One popular technique is the double treble crochet, which is a taller stitch that creates a more open and lacy effect. To work a double treble crochet, yarn over three times and then insert your hook into the stitch you want to work into. Yarn over and pull the loop through the stitch, leaving four loops on your hook. Yarn over again and pull the loop through the first two loops on your hook, leaving three loops. Yarn over again and pull the loop through the next two loops on your hook, leaving two loops. Yarn over again and pull the loop through the last two loops on your hook, completing the stitch.

Another advanced technique is the popcorn stitch, which creates a raised, textured effect. To work a popcorn stitch, work five double crochet stitches into the same stitch or space. Remove your hook from the last stitch and insert it into the top of the first double crochet stitch. Yarn over and pull the loop through the stitch, completing the popcorn stitch.

Tips and Tricks

To help ensure your filet crochet projects look their best, there are a few tips and tricks you can follow. First, it is important to choose the right yarn and hook for your project. A smooth, medium-weight yarn and a size G or H hook are good choices for beginners.

Second, it is important to pay attention to your tension as you crochet. This will help ensure your stitches are even and consistent, which will make your project look better overall. If your stitches are too tight, your fabric will be stiff and inflexible. If they are too loose, your fabric will be loose and saggy.

Finally, it is a good idea to practice your filet crochet skills on a small project before tackling a larger one. This will help you get a feel for the technique and build your confidence.

Filet crochet is a beautiful and versatile type of crochet that can be used to create a wide range of designs and patterns. With a few basic materials and tools, along with some practice and patience, anyone can learn to crochet with filet. Whether you are a beginner or an experienced crocheter, filet crochet is a rewarding and satisfying technique that is well worth exploring.

Chapter 31: Learning Tunisian Crochet

Tunisian crochet is one of the most popular crochet techniques that originated from Tunisia. It is a type of crochet that uses a long hook to make a dense and sturdy fabric. The technique is similar to knitting and crocheting, but it is done on a different type of hook.

Tunisian crochet has become more and more popular in recent years, and there is an increasing demand for people to learn this skill. In this chapter, we will look at what Tunisian crochet is, the different types of stitches used, and how to get started.

What is Tunisian Crochet?

Tunisian crochet is a technique that uses a long crochet hook to stitch loops onto the hook. Unlike regular crochet, you keep all the loops on the hook until you complete the row. This means that the fabric you create is thicker and stiffer than regular crochet.

One of the unique features of Tunisian crochet is that you can create a range of intricate patterns and shapes with the different stitches. You can even create designs that resemble knitting, which is why Tunisian crochet is sometimes called "the hybrid of knit and crochet."

The History of Tunisian Crochet

The exact origins of Tunisian crochet are not clear, but it is believed to have originated in Tunisia in the mid-19th century. The technique was initially used to create fabrics for clothing and household objects, but it gradually became an art form in its own right.

Over the years, Tunisian crochet has spread to other countries, and different variations of the technique have developed. In the United States, it is often referred to as "afghan crochet."

The Basics of Tunisian Crochet

Before you start with Tunisian crochet, you need to have a few basic tools. You will need a Tunisian crochet hook, which is longer than a regular crochet hook, and some yarn.

The basic technique for Tunisian crochet involves two main steps: the forward pass and the return pass. Here is how you do them:

The Forward Pass

1. Chain a number of stitches to your desired width.
2. Insert the hook in the second chain from the hook.
3. Yarn over and pull up a loop. Leave the loop on your hook.
4. Repeat step 3 for each chain until you reach the end of the row.
5. Keep all the loops on the hook.

The Return Pass

1. Yarn over and pull through one loop on the hook.

2. Yarn over and pull through two loops on the hook.
3. Repeat step 2 until you reach the end of the row.

Now that you know the basics of Tunisian crochet, you can start to explore the different stitches that you can use to create different patterns and textures.

The Different Stitches in Tunisian Crochet

Tunisian crochet offers a range of stitches that you can use to create all kinds of patterns and textures. Here are some of the most common stitches in Tunisian crochet:

1. Tunisian Simple Stitch (TSS)
The Tunisian Simple Stitch is the most basic stitch in Tunisian crochet. It creates a dense, tight fabric that is ideal for items like bags, blankets, and jackets. Here is how you do it:

1. Insert the hook in the second vertical bar from the hook.
2. Yarn over and pull up a loop. Leave the loop on your hook.
3. Repeat step 2 for each vertical bar until you reach the end of the row.
4. Use the return pass to finish the row.

2. Tunisian Knit Stitch (TKS)
The Tunisian Knit Stitch creates a fabric that looks like it was made using knitting needles. It is an attractive stitch that is ideal for

clothing, scarves, and hats. Here is how you do it:

1. Insert the hook between the front and back vertical bars of the previous stitch.
2. Yarn over and pull up a loop. Leave the loop on your hook.
3. Repeat step 2 for each stitch until you reach the end of the row.
4. Use the return pass to finish the row.

3. Tunisian Purl Stitch (TPS)
The Tunisian Purl Stitch creates a fabric that looks like it was made using the purl stitch in knitting. It is a bumpy stitch that adds texture to your work. Here is how you do it:

1. Bring the yarn in front of the hook.
2. Insert the hook in the front vertical bar of the previous stitch from right to left.
3. Yarn over and pull up a loop. Leave the loop on your hook.
4. Repeat step 3 for each stitch until you reach the end of the row.
5. Use the return pass to finish the row.

4. Tunisian Full Stitch (TFS)
The Tunisian Full Stitch creates a lacy fabric that is ideal for shawls and other lightweight items. Here is how you do it:

1. Yarn over and insert the hook in the second vertical bar from the hook.
2. Yarn over and pull up a loop. Leave the loop on your hook.

3. Yarn over again and insert the hook in the next vertical bar.
4. Yarn over and pull up a loop. Leave the loop on your hook.
5. Repeat steps 3 and 4 until you reach the end of the row.
6. Use the return pass to finish the row.

5. Tunisian Crochet Rib Stitch

The Tunisian Crochet Rib Stitch creates a stretchy, flexible fabric that is ideal for cuffs, collars, and hemlines. Here is how you do it:

1. Chain a multiple of two stitches.
2. TSS in the first stitch.
3. *TPS in the next stitch, TSS in the next stitch.*
4. Repeat step 3 until you reach the end of the row.
5. Use the return pass to finish the row.

As you become more familiar with Tunisian crochet, you can start to experiment with different stitch combinations to create your own unique designs.

Getting Started with Tunisian Crochet

If you're new to Tunisian crochet, the best way to get started is to practice the basic stitches until you feel confident. You can use scrap yarn if you don't want to waste any good yarn.

Once you're comfortable with the basics, you can start experimenting with different stitches and patterns. There are many online resources, including videos, tutorials, and patterns, that can help you learn more about Tunisian crochet.

Learning Tunisian crochet is a fun and rewarding experience. With a range of different stitches and patterns available, you can create all kinds of unique designs. By taking the time to practice and learn the basics, you can master this technique and create beautiful, handmade items that you can be proud of.

Chapter 32: Exploring Different Crochet Styles

When it comes to crochet, there are countless styles and techniques to choose from. Each style offers its own unique set of benefits and challenges, allowing crochet enthusiasts to experiment and find their niche in the craft. In this chapter, we will examine a few of the most popular crochet styles and discuss the characteristics, benefits, and challenges that come with each.

Amigurumi

Amigurumi is a style of crochet that is focused on creating small, stuffed toys and figurines. This style has gained a lot of popularity in recent years, particularly in the world of social media and online crafting communities. What sets Amigurumi apart from other crochet styles is its use of single crochet stitches and techniques to create three-dimensional shapes.

One of the benefits of Amigurumi is that it allows for a lot of creativity and personalization. There are endless possibilities for customizing the shape, size, and colors of your figures. Additionally, because Amigurumi projects are typically small and simple, they make great beginner projects.

However, Amigurumi can also be challenging for some crocheters. Because the focus is on creating three-dimensional shapes, it can be tricky to get the proportions just right. Additionally, the small size of these projects means that crocheting them can be physically uncomfortable for some people.

Filet Crochet

Filet crochet is a style that uses a mesh-like pattern to create intricate designs and shapes. It is particularly popular for creating home decor items such as curtains, table runners, and wall hangings. To create filet crochet, you will need to work a base of chain stitches and then fill in the mesh with double crochet stitches.

One of the benefits of filet crochet is its versatility. You can create a wide range of designs and patterns by changing the arrangement of the mesh and the double crochet stitches. Additionally, filet crochet projects tend to be very lightweight and drapey, which makes them great for home decor items.

However, filet crochet can also be challenging because of the intricate nature of the designs. It can be difficult to keep track of the pattern, especially if you are working on a large project. Additionally, because filet crochet uses a lot of open spaces, it may not be the best choice for projects that need to be sturdy or warm.

Tapestry Crochet

Tapestry crochet is a style that uses multiple colors of yarn to create complex designs and patterns. This style is often used for creating accessories such as bags, hats, and mittens. Tapestry crochet involves working with multiple strands of yarn at the same time, which requires some coordination and practice.

One of the benefits of tapestry crochet is its endless potential for creativity. You can create almost any design you can imagine by using different color combinations and stitch patterns. Additionally, because tapestry crochet projects tend to use thicker yarns, they can be very durable and warm.

However, tapestry crochet can also be challenging. It can be difficult to keep the tension consistent when working with multiple strands of yarn, which can lead to uneven or misshapen projects. Additionally, because of the color changes and design complexity, tapestry crochet projects can be time-consuming and require a lot of focus.

Bavarian Crochet

Bavarian crochet, also known as the Royal Albert stitch, is a style that uses a series of double crochet clusters to create a unique, textured fabric. This style is often used for creating blankets, shawls, and other cozy accessories. Unlike other crochet styles, Bavarian crochet does not use a traditional stitch pattern, but instead relies on a repeating set of clusters.

One of the benefits of Bavarian crochet is its ability to create a thick, warm fabric that is perfect for cold-weather projects. Additionally, because this style does not rely on a traditional stitch pattern, it can be easy to memorize and work quickly.

However, Bavarian crochet can also be challenging for some crocheters. Because it relies heavily on double crochet clusters, it can be easy to lose track of where you are in the pattern. Additionally, the clusters can sometimes be difficult to work through, which can make the fabric feel stiff or bulky.

These are just a few of the many crochet styles that exist in the world of crafting. Each style offers its own unique set of benefits and challenges, allowing crocheters to experiment and find their niche in the craft. Whether you prefer the intricate details of filet crochet or the colorful creativity of tapestry crochet, there is a crochet style out there that is perfect for you. So why not try something new and explore the endless possibilities of crochet today?

Chapter 33: Introduction to Amigurumi

If you're a fan of cute and colorful figures, then you've probably come across amigurumi before. Whether you've seen pictures on social media or bought a piece at a craft fair, amigurumi has become a beloved art form. But what exactly is amigurumi, and how did it all start? In this chapter, we'll take a closer look at this adorable trend, its origins, and how you can get started making your own amigurumi projects.

What is Amigurumi?

Amigurumi is a Japanese term that translates to "crocheted or knitted stuffed toy." Typically, these toys are small, soft, and made of yarn. They're known for their unique and whimsical designs, which often include animals, creatures, and cartoon characters. Amigurumi can be made using a range of techniques, including crocheting, knitting, needle felting, and sewing.

Origins of Amigurumi

The origins of amigurumi can be traced back to Japan in the 1980s. At the time, amigurumi was a niche craft that was popular among women. It wasn't until the early 2000s that amigurumi started gaining popularity worldwide, thanks in part to the rise of social media.

One of the early pioneers of amigurumi was designer and author, Saori Yamazaki. Her book, "Natural Cute Amigurumi," published in 2002, helped popularize amigurumi and introduced new techniques and styles to the craft.

Another influential figure in the world of amigurumi is designer and author, Kyoko Nemoto. Her book, "Cuddly Crochet," published in 2005, introduced amigurumi to a wider audience and helped make it a worldwide phenomenon.

How to Make Amigurumi

Now that you know a little bit about amigurumi, let's take a look at how you can make your own cute and cuddly creatures. Here's a basic guide to get you started:

Materials

To make amigurumi, you'll need a few basic materials:

- Yarn: Choose a soft and flexible yarn, such as cotton or acrylic. You can use any color or combination of colors that you like.
- Crochet hook: Choose a size that works with your chosen yarn. A smaller hook will give you a tighter stitch, while a larger hook will give you a looser stitch.
- Stuffing: Choose a soft and lightweight stuffing, such as polyester fiberfill.

- Tapestry needle: Use this to sew the pieces of your amigurumi together and to weave in ends.

Pattern

Once you have your materials together, you'll need a pattern to follow. You can find amigurumi patterns in books, online, or by designing your own. Make sure to choose a pattern that matches your skill level and interest.

Crochet Techniques

There are a few crochet techniques that are used to make amigurumi. These include:

- Magic Ring: This technique is used to start your amigurumi with a tight, closed circle. Check out this tutorial from All About Ami for step-by-step instructions.
- Single Crochet: This is the most common stitch used in amigurumi. It creates a tight, sturdy stitch that is perfect for stuffing.
- Increase: This stitch is used to add stitches to your project and make it wider. It's typically written in patterns as "sc 2 in next st."
- Decrease: This stitch is used to remove stitches from your project and make it narrower. It's typically written in patterns as "sc2tog."

Assembly

Once you have all of your pieces crocheted, it's time to assemble your amigurumi. Use a tapestry needle and matching yarn to sew the pieces together. Be sure to stuff your amigurumi as you go, being careful not to overstuff.

Finishing

Once your amigurumi is sewn together, you can add finishing touches, such as eyes, noses, and small details. There are many different ways to add these details, including safety eyes, embroidery, and felt.

Tips for Making Amigurumi

Here are a few tips to keep in mind as you start making amigurumi:

- Choose a small hook: Using a small hook will give you a tighter stitch, which is important for stuffing your amigurumi.
- Use stitch markers: Use stitch markers to keep track of your stitches and increases and decreases. You can use a safety pin, paper clip, or piece of yarn as a marker.
- Stuff carefully: Be careful not to overstuff your amigurumi, as it can make it look lumpy or misshapen.
- Practice, practice, practice: Like any new skill, amigurumi takes practice. Start with a simple pattern and work your way up to more complex designs.

Amigurumi is a fun and rewarding craft that has grown in popularity worldwide. With a few basic materials and some crochet skills, you can create your own adorable and cuddly toys. Whether you're a beginner or an experienced crafter, the possibilities are endless with amigurumi.

Chapter 34: Crochet Project: Amigurumi Teddy Bear

Crochet is not just a hobby, but it is also a form of art and skill that can bring joy to many people. One of the most popular genres of crochet is amigurumi, which is the Japanese art of crocheting small, stuffed creatures. Amigurumi is a combination of two words: "ami" which means "crocheted" or "knitted," and "nuigurumi" which means "stuffed doll."

In this chapter, we will learn about a crochet project: Amigurumi Teddy Bear. A teddy bear is a classic toy that has been around for over a century and is universally loved by children and adults alike. It is no wonder that there are many patterns available to make amigurumi teddy bears.

Materials

Before we start crocheting, we need to gather the materials. Here is a list of what we will need:

- Worsted weight yarn in two colors. You can choose any color you like, but brown and cream are the most popular colors for teddy bears.
- A 3.5 mm crochet hook. You can use a different size hook, but the size of the bear will be affected.
- Stuffing material. You can use polyester fiberfill or any other stuffing material you prefer.

- Scissors
- Yarn needle
- Stitch marker

Chapter 3: Pattern

Now that we have all the materials, it is time to start crocheting. Here is the pattern we will be using:

Head

Round 1: Magic circle 6 stitches.

Round 2: 2 sc in each stitch around. (12 stitches)

Round 3: *1 sc in the next stitch, 2 sc in the next stitch.* Repeat from * to * around. (18 stitches)

Round 4: *1 sc in the next 2 stitches, 2 sc in the next stitch.* Repeat from * to * around. (24 stitches)

Round 5: *1 sc in the next 3 stitches, 2 sc in the next stitch.* Repeat from * to * around. (30 stitches)

Round 6: *1 sc in the next 4 stitches, 2 sc in the next stitch.* Repeat from * to * around. (36 stitches)

Round 7 - 11: 1 sc in each stitch around.

Round 12: *1 sc in the next 4 stitches, sc2tog.* Repeat from * to * around. (30 stitches)

Round 13: *1 sc in the next 3 stitches, sc2tog.* Repeat from * to * around. (24 stitches)

Round 14: *1 sc in the next 2 stitches, sc2tog.* Repeat from * to * around. (18 stitches)

Round 15: *1 sc in the next stitch, sc2tog.* Repeat from * to * around. (12 stitches)

Stuff the head.

Round 16: Sc2tog around. (6 stitches)

Fasten off and sew the remaining stitches together.

Body

Round 1: Magic circle 6 stitches.

Round 2: 2 sc in each stitch around. (12 stitches)

Round 3: *1 sc in the next stitch, 2 sc in the next stitch.* Repeat from

* to * around. (18 stitches)

Round 4: *1 sc in the next 2 stitches, 2 sc in the next stitch.* Repeat from * to * around. (24 stitches)

Round 5: *1 sc in the next 3 stitches, 2 sc in the next stitch.* Repeat from * to * around. (30 stitches)

Round 6 - 9: 1 sc in each stitch around.

Round 10: *1 sc in the next 3 stitches, sc2tog.* Repeat from * to * around. (24 stitches)

Round 11: *1 sc in the next 2 stitches, sc2tog.* Repeat from * to * around. (18 stitches)

Stuff the body.

Round 12: *1 sc in the next stitch, sc2tog.* Repeat from * to * around. (12 stitches)

Fasten off and leave a long tail for sewing.

Arms (make 2)

Round 1: Magic circle 6 stitches.

Round 2 - 4: 1 sc in each stitch around.

Fasten off and leave a long tail for sewing.

Legs (make 2)

Round 1: Magic circle 6 stitches.

Round 2 - 6: 1 sc in each stitch around.

Fasten off and leave a long tail for sewing.

Ears (make 2)

Round 1: Magic circle 6 stitches.

Round 2: 2 sc in each stitch around. (12 stitches)

Round 3: *1 sc in the next stitch, 2 sc in the next stitch.* Repeat from * to * around. (18 stitches)

Round 4: 1 sc in each stitch around.

Fasten off and leave a long tail for sewing.

Assembly

1. Sew the head to the body using the long tail left from the body.

2. Sew the arms and legs to the body.

3. Sew the ears to the head.

4. Use black yarn to embroider the eyes and nose.

Your Amigurumi Teddy Bear is now complete!

Chapter 35: Using Stitch Markers in Crochet

As crocheters, we often have to juggle multiple tasks at once, from following a pattern to keeping track of stitch counts. This can become overwhelming and lead to mistakes in our work. Thankfully, stitch markers are here to help!

Stitch markers are small, often colorful, rings or clips that are placed on the crochet project during the stitching process to mark specific stitches or points in the pattern. They can be a lifesaver when following difficult or complex patterns, or when working on larger projects that require the use of multiple stitch counts.

In this chapter, we will explore the different types of stitch markers, how to use them correctly, and some tips and tricks to help you get the most out of these invaluable tools.

Types of Stitch Markers

Stitch markers come in a variety of shapes, sizes, and materials. Here are some of the most commonly used types:

- Ring stitch markers: These are small, circular rings that can be clipped onto a stitch. They are ideal for marking a specific stitch in the pattern, or for identifying the beginning or end of a round.
- Locking stitch markers: These have a more secure hold than ring stitch markers and are ideal for marking a specific stitch or place in

the pattern that you need to remember and count as you go.
- Split-ring stitch markers: These are similar to ring stitch markers, but they have a small split in the ring, allowing them to be opened and closed. They are ideal for marking a specific stitch count in the pattern, or for marking the beginning or end of a row.
- Bulb pins: These are long, curved pins with a bulb-shaped head. They are ideal for marking a specific stitch, or for keeping track of increases or decreases in the pattern.
- Paperclips: Yes, you read that correctly! Regular office supply paperclips can be used as stitch markers in a pinch. Simply bend them into a circle shape and clip them onto your project.

Choosing the right stitch marker can depend on the project you are working on and personal preference. Experiment with different types to find what works best for you.

Using Stitch Markers

Once you have selected your stitch markers, it's time to start using them. Here are some tips to get you started:

- Read the pattern: Before starting your project, read the pattern and identify where stitch markers are needed. They will often be mentioned in the pattern notes or directions.
- Count carefully: Make sure you have the correct number of stitches in the correct places before placing your stitch markers. This will help ensure that your project is symmetrical and uniform.

- Place the markers correctly: Always place the stitch markers on the stitch, not the space between stitches. This will ensure that they do not accidentally fall off.
- Keep track of stitch counts: As you work through the pattern, keep track of your stitch counts with your stitch markers. This will help you identify any errors early on and avoid having to unravel your work later.
- Remove the markers as you go: As you crochet, remove stitch markers as you come to them in the pattern. This will prevent them from getting tangled in your work or slipping off accidentally.

Tips and tricks

Here are some additional tips and tricks for using stitch markers:

- Use different colors: If you are working on a pattern with multiple stitch counts or repeats, use different colored stitch markers to help you keep track of each section.
- Use stitch markers to identify changes: If you are working on a project that requires color changes or stitch pattern changes, use stitch markers to mark the places where you need to make the change.
- Place stitch markers on the wrong side of the work: If you are working on a project where the right and wrong sides look similar, place stitch markers on the wrong side of the work to help you distinguish between the two.
- Use stitch markers for more than just crochet: Stitch markers can

also be helpful for other types of needlework, such as knitting, embroidery, and cross-stitch. Keep a few on hand to use for all your crafting needs.

Stitch markers are an invaluable tool for any crocheter, whether you are a beginner or an experienced crafter. They can help you keep track of stitch counts, identify important places in the pattern, and prevent mistakes in your work. Experiment with different types of stitch markers and techniques to find what works best for you and your project. Happy crocheting!

Chapter 36: Understanding Yarn Dye Lots

One of the most important aspects of working with yarn is understanding dye lots. When you purchase a skein of yarn, it is important to take note of the dye lot number and to make sure that all of the skeins you purchase for a particular project come from the same dye lot. Why is this so important? Let's take a closer look.

What is a Dye Lot?

A dye lot is a batch of yarn that has been dyed at the same time and with the same dye formula. Each batch of yarn will have its own unique dye lot number. This number is usually printed on the label of the yarn and identifies the specific batch of yarn that the skein came from.

Why do Different Dye Lots Matter?

The color of a skein of yarn can vary slightly from one dye lot to the next. The difference may be very subtle or quite noticeable, depending on the yarn and the dyeing process. If you use a skein of yarn from one dye lot in the middle of a project that was started with another dye lot, the color change might be quite noticeable. This can result in an unattractive seam where the two dye lots meet.

When purchasing yarn, take care to ensure that all of the skeins you buy are from the same dye lot, especially if you are starting a new project. If you need to buy more yarn later, make sure to check the dye lot number on the new skeins to make sure they match the original batch.

How are Dye Lots Determined?

When yarn is dyed, the dyeing process is carefully controlled to ensure that all the skeins in a batch are as close in color as possible. The dye lot number is assigned based on the date and time that the yarn was dyed and the specific dye formula that was used.

Most manufacturers will keep detailed records of their dyeing process so that they can reproduce the same colors consistently from batch to batch. However, variations can still occur, especially if the yarn is dyed by hand or if natural dyes are used.

How to Check Dye Lots

To check the dye lot of a skein of yarn, simply look for the dye lot number on the label. If you are purchasing yarn in store, it should be easy to find the dye lot number on the label or package. If you are purchasing yarn online, make sure to read the product description carefully to ensure that you are purchasing yarn from the correct dye lot.

If you are in doubt about whether two skeins of yarn are from the same dye lot, you can compare the colors side by side. Hold the balls of yarn next to each other and look for any differences in color. If you can see a difference, the skeins are from different dye lots and should not be used together in the same project.

If you are working with a multi-colored yarn, it may be difficult to tell whether all of the colors in the different skeins match exactly. In this case, it is a good idea to alternate between skeins while working on your project to avoid any noticeable color differences.

What To Do if You Can't Find the Same Dye Lot

It is always best to use yarn from the same dye lot for a project, but sometimes it is simply not possible. If you can't find the same dye lot and need to use a different batch of yarn, there are a few things you can do to minimize any noticeable color differences.

First, try to find yarn that is as close in color to the original as possible. If the color difference is subtle, you may be able to make it work by alternating between the two dye lots while you work on your project.

If the color difference is more noticeable, you may need to use the different dye lot in a way that minimizes the appearance of the color difference. For example, if you are making a sweater, you could use the different dye lot for the sleeves or collar instead of the body of the sweater.

In some cases, you may be able to solve the problem by knitting or crocheting with two strands of yarn held together. This will help to blend the two colors together and create a more cohesive look.

Understanding dye lots is an important aspect of working with yarn. Taking the time to carefully check the dye lot numbers on the skeins of yarn you purchase can help to avoid any unwanted surprises in your finished project. While it is always best to use yarn from the same dye lot, there are ways to work with multiple dye lots to minimize any color differences. With a little bit of knowledge and care, you can create beautiful, cohesive projects with any skein of yarn.

Chapter 37: Care Instructions for Crochet Items

Crochet items are becoming increasingly popular in our daily lives. They add a touch of creativity and individuality to our homes, wardrobes, and gifts that we give. Crochet is not an easy art, and it demands time, patience, attention to detail, and creativity. When it comes to maintaining crochet items, it is essential to know how to take care of them. The care instructions for crochet items vary depending upon the fiber content and type of stitch used. In this chapter, we will discuss the care instructions for crochet items that will keep them looking new for years.

Understanding Fiber Content

Fiber content plays a vital role in determining the care that crochet items require. Common fiber contents used in crochet are cotton, wool, acrylic, and blends of various fibers. Understanding these fibers is crucial in choosing the right washing, drying, and storage method for your items.

Cotton Crochet Items: Cotton crochet items are breathable, absorbent, and durable. These items can be machine-washed with a gentle cycle in cold water. If the product has any dirt or stains, it is advisable to soak it before washing. Bleach should also be avoided as it can weaken the fibers. The best way to dry cotton crochet items is to lay them flat on a towel and reshape them if required. Cotton items that are hung to dry often stretch and lose their shape.

Wool Crochet Items: Wool crochet items are warm, soft, and lightweight. However, they require special attention when it comes to washing and drying. Wool is a delicate fiber that can shrink or felt if not washed carefully. Handwashing wool crochet items is the best way to ensure their longevity. Use a mild soap in cold water and avoid agitation. Gently squeeze the water out of the item and lay it flat on a towel to dry. Avoid hanging wool crochet items as they can lose their shape and become distorted.

Acrylic Crochet Items: Acrylic is a man-made fiber that resembles wool but is more affordable and durable. Acrylic crochet items can be machine-washed in cold water with a gentle cycle, but it is recommended to wash them separately. Fabric softeners should be avoided as it can cause the fibers to pill. When drying acrylic crochet items, place them in a dryer with a delicate cycle or lay them flat on a towel.

Blended Fiber Crochet Items: Blended fiber crochet items contain a combination of two or more fibers. It is essential to understand the fiber content and follow the care instructions accordingly.

Washing and Drying Crochet Items

Washing and drying crochet items is crucial to their longevity. Here are some general guidelines to follow when washing and drying crochet items:

1. Always read the care instructions on the yarn label or pattern label before washing your crochet item.

2. Avoid using hot water as it can damage the fibers.

3. Use a mild detergent that is suitable for delicate fibers.

4. Avoid fabric softeners as they can weaken the fibers.

5. Do not wring or twist the item as it can cause it to lose its shape.

6. Do not hang crochet items as it can cause stretching.

7. Lay the item flat on a towel and reshape it if required.

8. Avoid using a dryer if possible, as heat can damage fibers.

Chapter 4: Storing Crochet Items

Proper storage is crucial to protect crochet items from dust, dirt, and moths. Here are some tips to store crochet items:

1. Clean the item before storing it.

2. Place the item in a fabric storage bag or a pillowcase, avoiding plastic bags as they can trap moisture.

3. Add a sachet of lavender or cedar to the storage bag to deter moths.

4. Store crochet items in a cool and dry place, avoiding direct sunlight or damp areas.

Crochet items are becoming increasingly popular, and it is essential to take care of them to ensure their longevity. Understanding the fiber content and following the appropriate washing, drying, and storage instructions is crucial to keep the items looking new for years. By following these simple guidelines, you can enjoy your crochet items for years to come.

Chapter 38: Organizing Your Crochet Supplies

Crochet is one of the most popular crafting hobbies around the world. It is a fun and relaxing way to create beautiful items, from cozy blankets to stylish garments and accessories. While the process of crocheting can be enjoyable, keeping your crochet supplies organized can be a challenge. A messy and disorganized workspace can make it difficult to find the right tools and materials, slow down your progress, and even discourage you from working on projects. In this chapter, we will share some essential tips and tricks to help you organize your crochet supplies and make your crafting experience more enjoyable.

1. Start by decluttering

The first step in organizing your crochet supplies is to declutter. Go through all your crochet materials and tools and get rid of anything that is broken, outdated, or you no longer use. This includes old yarn, hooks with missing or damaged handles, and any other items that have seen better days. You can either throw away or donate these items.

2. Sort your materials

Once you have decluttered, sort your materials by type and color. This will make it easier to find what you need when you start a new project. You can use bins or containers to keep different yarns separated. Also, separate your yarns by color and weight. For example, keep all your worsted weight yarns together and separate your lighter weight yarns.

3. Keep your hooks organized

Hooks are the most important tool in crochet. It is essential to keep your hooks in good condition and easily accessible. Group your hooks by size and type and keep them in a case or organizer. You can use a hook case or make one of your own using a pencil case and some foam. Arrange the hooks by size and label the slots for easy replacement.

4. Label your yarns

It is beneficial to label your yarns by color and weight. You can use stick-on labels or tags. This will help you keep track of your yarn inventory and prevent confusion when starting a new project. You can also mark the labels with the date you purchased the yarn.

5. Use clear containers

Clear containers are an excellent way to store your crochet supplies. You can easily see what is inside, and it makes finding what you need more manageable. Use plastic containers for storage and label the containers according to the materials inside, such as yarn, safety eyes, stuffing, or fabric.

6. Utilize wall organizers

Wall organizers are an excellent way to free up space and keep your crochet supplies organized and easily accessible. You can use pegboard or wire baskets to store your yarns and hooks. Group your materials by color to create a beautiful and functional display. You can even display your finished projects on the wall for inspiration.

7. Keep a note-book

A notebook is handy to keep track of your crochet projects, ideas, and patterns. You can use a simple notebook or a planner designed for crafters. Make a list of the projects you want to make and the necessary materials. Write down any notes, ideas, or modifications you want to make.

8. Create a project basket

A project basket is an excellent way to keep your current project organized and easily portable. Use a small basket or tote bag and fill it with your yarn, hooks, pattern, and any other materials or tools you need for the project. Make sure to label the basket with the project name, pattern, and yarn type.

9. Keep your workspace clean

Finally, it is essential to keep your workspace clean and clutter-free.

Put away your supplies after each session, and tidy up your space. This will help you feel more organized and productive the next time you sit down to crochet.

Organizing your crochet supplies is an essential part of maintaining a successful and enjoyable crafting hobby. By decluttering, sorting your materials, organizing your hooks, labeling your yarns, using clear containers, wall organizers, keeping a notebook, creating a project basket, and keeping your workspace clean, you can create an organized and functional workspace and an overall successful crochet experience.

Chapter 39: Crocheting for Charity

Crocheting has been a beloved craft for centuries and has brought joy to many people with its intricacy and warmth. While many individuals crochet for personal reasons, there is also a growing trend of crocheting for charity. Charitable organizations across the world are actively seeking crocheted items for various causes and individuals are eager to lend their skills to aid those in need.

Charitable crochet organizations are dedicated to collecting crocheted items – from blankets and scarves to hats and toys – from generous individuals to distribute to populations in need. An example of a highly successful charitable crochet organization is the Knit for Peace group, which was founded in the UK in 2009. Knit for Peace takes in over 10,000 knitted and crocheted items a year, including knitted sweaters and crocheted blankets, which are then distributed to various charities and causes. The group's donations have benefitted a variety of causes, including refugees, homeless individuals, hospitals, and women in domestic abuse shelters.

Many other organizations, both large and small, have followed Knit for Peace's lead and have launched their own efforts to collect crocheted items for charitable purposes. For example, Warm Up America!, a US-based organization, has been accepting crocheted and knitted blankets to distribute to homeless shelters and disaster relief centers since 1991. Similarly, Crochet for Cancer, which was founded in 2011, encourages crocheters and knitters across the US to donate handmade items such as hats and scarves to cancer patients undergoing treatments. The organization collects thousands of items every year, providing hope and comfort to cancer patients and survivors.

One of the advantages of crocheting for charity is that it provides individuals with a sense of purpose and community. By dedicating time and effort to a charitable cause, crocheters are able to connect with like-minded people and contribute to a larger social cause. This sense of connection and purpose can be particularly important for those with chronic illnesses or disabilities, who may feel isolated or disconnected from their communities.

Crocheting for charity also provides a great opportunity for individuals to develop and improve their crocheting skills. This can happen in a variety of ways, including following new patterns, experimenting with new techniques, and exploring creative possibilities. Some organizations even offer free patterns and guidance, providing crocheters with additional resources and support to develop their skills.

Another benefit of crocheting for charity is that it allows crocheters to give back to their communities in a way that is both meaningful and tangible. The items that are created and donated, such as blankets, scarves, and hats, are often used for warmth and comfort, which can have a profound impact on the people who receive them. Knowing that their efforts have directly and positively impacted someone's life can be incredibly empowering and rewarding.

Crocheting for charity also allows individuals to use their craft to spread awareness and advocate for important causes. For example, several charities use crocheted items to raise awareness for specific issues. One such organization is The Innocent Big Knit, a UK-based group that collects knitted or crocheted hats to distribute to drinks with a portion of the proceeds going to Age UK, a charity that supports elderly individuals. The hats, which are placed on top of smoothie bottles sold in stores nationwide, serve as a reminder of the issues that elderly individuals face, such as loneliness and isolation.

Crocheting for charity can also have a positive impact on the environment. By creating reusable items such as shopping bags, face cloths, and dishcloths, crocheters are helping to reduce waste and promote sustainable living. These items can also serve as a reminder of the importance of conservation and environmental stewardship.

However, despite the many benefits of crocheting for charity, it is not without its challenges. One of the main challenges is finding reputable and effective organizations to donate crocheted items to. While there are many organizations dedicated to collecting crocheted items for charitable purposes, not all of them are credible or efficient. As a result, it is important for crocheters to do their research and find reputable organizations and causes to donate to.

Another challenge is ensuring that the items being donated are of high quality. While crocheting for charity is typically done with the best intentions, sometimes crocheters may not take enough care to ensure that the items being donated are of high quality. This can result in items that are poorly made or fall apart quickly, which defeats the purpose of donating for charitable purposes. To prevent this, it is important for crocheters to take their time and ensure that the items they are donating are well-made and durable.

Crocheting for charity is a powerful way for individuals to give back to their communities and support causes that are important to them. It provides crocheters with a sense of purpose and community, while also allowing them to develop their skills and advocate for important issues. While there are certainly challenges associated with crocheting for charity, the potential benefits – both for the crocheter and the people who receive the donated items – make it a worthwhile and rewarding endeavor.

Chapter 40: Making Crochet Gifts

Crochet is an amazing craft that has been in existence for centuries. It is a craft that requires creativity, time, and patience. It is perfect for creating a wide range of items from blankets to scarves, hats, and even toys. One of the best things about crochet is that it can be used to create unique and personalized gifts that are perfect for any occasion. In this chapter, we will explore the art of making crochet gifts, including the best patterns, materials, and techniques.

Why Crochet Gifts Are Special

The reason why crochet gifts are so important is that they are handmade. Unlike mass-produced products, crochet gifts are one-of-a-kind and are created with the recipient in mind. The love, effort, and time put into each stitch make them extra special and personal. This makes receiving a crochet gift something that is treasured and cherished for years to come.

Choosing the Right Pattern

The first step in creating a beautiful crochet gift is choosing the right pattern. The pattern should be chosen based on the recipient's interests and preferences. For example, if the recipient loves animals, consider creating a crochet stuffed animal. If they might love a cozy blanket, go for a pattern that creates the coziest blanket possible. Pinterest, Ravelry, or other websites are a great place to find inspiration.

Materials Matter

Choosing the right materials is also essential when making a crochet gift. It is important to choose the best quality yarn available. Yarn comes in different weights, colors, and textures, so choose the one that is perfect for the project. Make sure that the colors used complement one another and that the yarn is soft and comfortable. Also, consider the size of the project and choose the hook size accordingly.

Color Combination

In addition to the texture and quality of the yarn, color combination is also an important factor to consider. A poor color combination could ruin a beautiful pattern, while a perfect color combination could transform something average into something that's stunning. Don't be afraid to mix and match colors! Choose a color palette that works best for the project and enjoy your creativity.

Techniques for Creating Stunning Crochet Gifts

Once the pattern and materials have been selected, techniques for creating a stunning crochet gift come into play. The techniques used will depend on the project being created. For example, if it is a crochet stuffed animal, amigurumi technique will be required. For blankets, granny square motif may be the best choice.

Blocking Piece

One helpful technique that can be used in almost all crochet projects is blocking. Blocking is a process used to give the finished piece a more professional and polished look. To block a piece, the finished piece is dampened with water or steam, stretched gently to the desired size and shape, and then left to dry. This process helps to even out the stitches and give the final product a more polished look.

Finishing Touches

After all the stitches are finished, it is important to tidy up the final product neatly. Using a tapestry needle, weave in all loose ends of yarn left from cutting and trimming. The final piece will then be ready to be gifted to the receiver.

Creating crochet gifts is a fun and rewarding experience. Every piece made is an opportunity to show how much one cares about the recipient. By following the different techniques shared in this chapter, anyone can create personalized and unique crochet gifts that will be prized and cherished for years to come. With practice, patience, and creativity, one can become an expert at making beautiful crochet gifts. Happy crocheting!

Chapter 41: Selling Your Crochet Work

Crochet is a therapeutic and rewarding hobby that can also be a great way to make a little extra income. If you are a skilled crocheter and have a knack for creating beautiful items, then you might be interested in selling your crochet work.

In this chapter, we will explore the ins and outs of selling your crochet work, from choosing what to sell to setting a price that is fair for both you and your customers. We will also discuss some of the challenges that you may face when trying to sell your crochet work and provide tips for overcoming these challenges.

Choosing What to Sell

The first step in selling your crochet work is choosing what to sell. Consider the items that you enjoy making and that are in demand. Some popular crochet items include hats, scarves, blankets, and home decor items such as coasters and dishcloths.

It is also important to consider the materials that you will use. While acrylic yarn may be cheaper, luxury yarns like wool or alpaca can be more expensive but also add a touch of sophistication to your creations.

Another factor to consider when choosing what to sell is your target market. Consider whether you want to appeal to a niche market, such as eco-conscious buyers who prefer natural fibers, or whether you want to appeal to a wider audience.

Setting a Price

Setting a price for your crochet work can be tricky. You want to make sure that you are not undervaluing your work, but you also want to be competitive in the market.

One way to determine a fair price is to calculate the cost of your materials and the amount of time it takes to create the item. Add these costs together and then add a markup for your time and skill. For example, if it takes you three hours to make a hat and the materials cost $5, you might want to charge $25 for the hat ($5 for materials and $20 for your time).

Another way to set a fair price is to research the market and see what similar items are selling for. Keep in mind that your price should reflect the quality of your work and the materials you used.

Marketing Your Crochet Work

Once you have created your crochet items and set a price, it is time to market your work. There are many ways to market your crochet items, including online marketplaces, craft fairs, and social media.

Online marketplaces such as Etsy and Amazon Handmade are great places to sell your crochet items. These platforms allow you to create a shop and list your items for sale, and they take care of the payment processing and shipping.

Craft fairs are another great way to market your crochet work. These events are held throughout the year and offer a way for you to showcase your items in person. You can also use social media to promote your crochet work. Platforms like Instagram and Facebook allow you to reach a wider audience and connect with potential customers.

Challenges When Selling Crochet Work

While selling your crochet work can be rewarding, it is not without its challenges. One of the biggest challenges is competition. With so many people selling crochet items, it can be difficult to stand out in the market.

Another challenge is pricing. It can be difficult to determine a fair price for your work, especially if you are new to selling crochet items. You may also face challenges with shipping and handling, especially if you are selling items internationally.

Tips for Overcoming Challenges

To overcome these challenges, it is important to differentiate yourself from the competition. Consider creating unique items or using high-quality materials to set yourself apart.

You can also focus on providing excellent customer service, such as responding to inquiries in a timely manner and providing updates on shipping.

When it comes to pricing, consider offering discounts for bulk orders or creating promotions to encourage customers to purchase multiple items.

Finally, when it comes to shipping and handling, make sure that you have a clear understanding of the costs involved and factor these costs into your pricing.

Selling your crochet work can be a great way to make a little extra income while doing something that you love. By carefully choosing what to sell, setting a fair price, and marketing your items, you can overcome challenges and succeed in the market.

As with any business venture, it is important to stay informed and adapt to changing market conditions. By staying on top of trends and continuing to grow your skills, you can continue to grow your crochet business and take it to new heights.

Chapter 42: Introduction to Crochet Lace

Crochet lace is a type of lace that is made using the technique of crochet. Crochet is a form of needlework that involves using a hook and yarn or thread to make different stitches. Crochet lace is a delicate and intricate form of crochet, which requires skill and patience to create. Crochet lace can be used to embellish many items such as clothing, linens, and home décor. It is a beautiful and timeless craft that has been around for centuries.

Before beginning with crochet lace, you should be familiar with basic crochet stitches such as chain stitch, single crochet, and double crochet. If you are not familiar with them, it is best to learn them first. Once you have mastered these basic stitches, you can move on to more complex stitches used in crochet lace such as picot stitch, clusters stitch, and shell stitch.

Crochet hook sizes vary depending on the size of the yarn or thread used in the project. The size of the hook is important because it affects the gauge or tension of the stitches. A larger hook size will produce larger stitches, while a smaller hook produces smaller stitches. The crochet hook size is usually indicated on the yarn or thread label.

Crochet lace can be made using many types of yarn or thread, including cotton, silk, wool, and linen. The type of yarn or thread used in the project affects the overall look of the lace. A fine, delicate thread is best used for intricate lace patterns, while a thicker yarn may be used for larger lace patterns.

There are many different types of crochet lace patterns, each with its own unique look and level of difficulty. Some popular patterns include pineapple stitch, Irish crochet, and filet crochet. Pineapple stitch is a popular pattern that features a cluster of stitches that resemble a pineapple. Irish crochet is a style of lace that is created by attaching different motifs together, such as flowers and leaves. Filet crochet is a lace that is made by creating a mesh-like fabric with solid patterns worked into it.

Once you have chosen a pattern, it's time to begin the project. The first step is to create a foundation chain, which is the starting point for the lace pattern. It is important to make sure that the foundation chain is long enough for your project before beginning the first row.

Once the foundation chain is created, you can begin to work the stitches of the pattern. To create the lace pattern, you will need to follow the instructions carefully, paying close attention to stitch counts and the placement of each stitch. Depending on the pattern, there may be different types of stitches used, such as clusters, chains, and double crochet stitches.

The most important thing to remember when creating crochet lace is to take your time and work carefully. Crochet lace is a delicate craft, and mistakes can be difficult to fix once the work has progressed to a certain point. It is also important to keep tension consistent throughout the project, as inconsistent tension can cause the finished project to look uneven.

When you have completed the lace pattern, it is time to finish the project. This can involve blocking the piece to flatten and shape it, as well as weaving in any loose ends of thread or yarn. Blocking involves stretching the piece out to its desired shape and size, and then pinning it in place to dry. This process ensures that the piece will retain its shape and lay flat.

Crochet lace is a beautiful and rewarding craft that can be enjoyed by beginners and experienced crocheters alike. With a little patience and practice, anyone can create a stunning piece of lace that will be cherished for years to come.

Chapter 43: Crochet Project: Lace Doily

As a crocheter, there is nothing more satisfying than completing a lace doily. The delicate intricacies of the pattern and the intricate lacework together create a beautiful addition to any tabletop. Doilies have been around since the 17th century, and serve both a functional and decorative purpose, protecting furniture from scratches and creating a more elegant atmosphere. Here's a guide to help you create your very own crochet lace doily!

Before beginning, it's essential to choose the thread and hook size that suits your preferences. There are several sizes and types of thread available, and each will provide a different look and feel to your finished work. A fine crochet thread will produce a delicate looking doily, while a thicker thread will have a more substantial appearance. Generally, a size 10 or 20 crocheting thread is recommended for creating doilies, so find a color and size that suit your preference.

Once you have chosen the thread and hook, it's time to start crafting your beautiful lace doily. Here is a pattern for a simple circular doily that you can use as a reference:

Materials:
- Size 10 crocheting thread
- A crochet hook (Size 7 or 1.65mm is suggested)
- A tapestry needle

Pattern:
Round 1: Make a slip knot and chain 6 stitches. Slip stitch into the first chain stitch to form a ring.
Round 2: Chain 3 and double crochet ten times into the ring. Slip stitch in the top of the third chain to complete the round.
Round 3: Chain 6 and skip one double crochet stitch in the previous round. Double crochet twice into the next stitch. Repeat this pattern all around the circle. Slip stitch into the third chain loop to complete the round.
Round 4: Chain eight and slip stitch into the third-chain loop on the previous round. Chain four and double crochet three times into the next chain loop. Chain four and repeat this pattern all around the circle. Slip stitch into the fourth chain to complete the row.
Round 5: Chain three and double crochet twice into the next chain loop. Chain two and double crochet three times into the next chain loop. Chain two and repeat this pattern all around the circle. Slip stitch into the third chain to complete the row.
Round 6: Chain five and slip stitch into the space between the first and second double crochet of the previous round. Chain five and skip the next chain two loop. Double crochet two times in the space between the double crochet grouping. Chain two and repeat this pattern all around the circle. Slip stitch into the fourth chain to complete the row.
Round 7: Chain three and double crochet twice into the five-chain arch. Chain three and double crochet three times into the next five-chain arch. Chain three and repeat this pattern all around the circle. Slip stitch into the third chain to complete the row.

Round 8: Chain six and slip stitch into the third chain loop of the next three double crochet grouping. Chain six and double crochet twice into the five-chain arch. Chain six and repeat this pattern all around the circle. Slip stitch into the second chain to complete the row.
Round 9: Chain six and double crochet twice into the six-chain arch. Chain six and slip stitch into the third chain of the next three double crochets. Chain six and repeat this pattern all around the circle. Slip stitch into the second chain to complete the row.
Round 10: Chain five and slip stitch into the sixth-chain arch. Chain five and double crochet twice into the six-chain arch. Chain five and repeat this pattern all around the circle. Slip stitch into the third chain to complete the row.
Round 11: Chain 10 and slip stitch into the fifth chain loop of the next group. Chain 13 and repeat this pattern all around the circle. Slip stitch into the fifth chain to complete the row.
Round 12: Chain six and double crochet twice into the ten-chain loop. Chain six and slip stitch into the second chain of the next thirteen-chain loop. Chain six and repeat this pattern all around the circle. Slip stitch into the second chain to complete the row.
Round 13: Chain six and slip stitch into the sixth chain loop. Chain six and double crochet twice into the ten-chain loop. Chain six and repeat this pattern all around the circle. Slip stitch into the second chain to complete the row.
Round 14: Chain eight and slip stitch into the sixth chain loop. Chain eight and double crochet twice into the six-chain loop. Chain eight and repeat this pattern all around the circle. Slip stitch into the fourth chain to complete the row.

Round 15: Chain five and double crochet into the space created between the two arches for the previous row. Chain two and double crochet again into the same space. Chain two and repeat this pattern all around the circle. Slip stitch into the third chain to complete the row.

Round 16: Chain three and single crochet twice into the two-chain loop. Chain two and single crochet thrice into the next two-chain loop. Chain two and repeat this pattern all around the circle. Slip stitch in the first single crochet to complete the row.

Round 17: Chain six and single crochet twice into the two-chain loop. Chain eight and single crochet three times into the next two-chain loop. Chain eight and repeat this pattern all around the circle. Slip stitch in the first single crochet to complete the row.

Round 18: Chain six and single crochet twice into the two-chain loop. Chain eleven and single crochet three times into the next two-chain loop. Chain eleven and repeat this pattern all around the circle. Slip stitch in the first single crochet to complete the row.

Round 19: Chain six and single crochet twice into the two-chain loop, chain 13 and single crochet three times into the two-chain loop. Chain 13 and repeat this pattern all around the circle. Slip stitch in the first single crochet to complete the row.

Round 20: Slip stitch into the first 13-chain loop and chain 8. Single crochet four times into the next two-single crochet loop. Chain eight and single crochet four times into the next two-single crochet loop. Repeat this pattern all around the circle. Slip stitch into the fifth chain to complete the row.

Your beautiful lace doily is now complete! This doily design is unique, but there are many lace doily patterns available out there, and you can use this pattern as a guide to help you create something that is entirely your own. If you're feeling ambitious, you can also choose different shapes and sizes, such as hexagonal, square, or rectangular doilies.

Crocheting a lace doily is a fulfilling project that will leave you with a beautiful piece of art that you can use to decorate your home or give as a gift. By choosing the right thread and hook size, using a simple lace doily pattern, and following the instructions carefully, you can create a stunning work of art that will be cherished for years to come.

Chapter 44: Exploring Advanced Crochet Techniques

Crochet is an incredibly versatile and rewarding craft, with techniques and patterns suitable for everyone from beginners to seasoned experts. Once you have mastered the basics of crochet, it is time to explore some more advanced techniques that will help you to create beautiful, complex designs. In this chapter, we will explore some of the most interesting and challenging crochet techniques, including lacework, filet crochet, Tunisian crochet, and tapestry crochet.

Lacework

Lacework is a traditional crochet technique that is used to create delicate, intricate patterns that resemble lace. Lacework crochet is typically done using fine, lightweight yarns and small hooks, allowing you to create incredibly detailed and intricate designs. Some of the most common stitches used in lacework crochet include the picot, the chain stitch, and the double crochet stitch.

One of the most important things to keep in mind when working on lacework crochet is to maintain an even tension throughout your work. This can be challenging when working with fine yarn and small hooks, but it is essential to ensure that your work looks neat and even.

Filet Crochet

Filet crochet is an interesting and challenging technique that involves creating a grid of crochet stitches, which are then used to form a pattern or image. In filet crochet, the stitches are typically created using double crochet or treble crochet stitches, creating a dense, sturdy fabric with plenty of texture.

One of the most interesting things about filet crochet is that it allows you to create complex, detailed images using just a few stitches. By varying the density of your stitches, you can create light and dark areas that help to give your image depth and dimension.

Tunisian Crochet

Tunisian crochet is an unusual and highly versatile crochet technique that combines elements of both crochet and knitting. In Tunisian crochet, you use a long hook with a stopper at one end to create a unique fabric that looks like a combination of knit and crochet.

One of the most interesting things about Tunisian crochet is that it allows you to create incredibly dense, warm fabrics with a lot of texture. By varying the size of your hook and the tension of your stitches, you can create fabrics that are suitable for a wide range of different projects.

Tapestry Crochet

Tapestry crochet is a technique that allows you to create complex, multi-colored designs using a single piece of yarn. This is achieved by carrying different colors of yarn across the back of your work, effectively creating a floating pattern that appears on the right side of your fabric.

One of the most challenging aspects of tapestry crochet is managing the tension of your yarn as you work. You need to ensure that you are not pulling your yarn too tightly or too loosely, otherwise, you may end up with uneven stitches or a distorted design.

Exploring advanced crochet techniques is a great way to take your craft to the next level and create truly beautiful, intricate designs. Whether you are interested in lacework, filet crochet, Tunisian crochet, or tapestry crochet, there are plenty of techniques and patterns to choose from. By taking the time to practice and perfect these advanced techniques, you can create stunning, unique creations that are sure to impress. So why not take the plunge and try your hand at some of these exciting and challenging techniques today?

Chapter 45: Creating Your Own Crochet Patterns

Crochet is an art that allows you to express your creativity, and creating your own crochet patterns is an opportunity to leave your personal touch. Making your own patterns is an excellent way to experiment with stitches, shapes, and colors and bring your ideas to life. Although it might seem daunting to design your own crochet pattern, it is achievable with some patience, practice, and a little bit of guidance. This chapter will take you through the process of creating your own crochet pattern.

Getting Started

To start creating your own crochet pattern, you need to have an idea of what you would like to make. Your inspiration can come from many different sources such as a flower in your garden, a picture on the internet or in a book, or an item of clothing that you would like to replicate.

Once you have an idea in mind, you can start to sketch it out on paper. Sketching out your design can help you visualize the stitches and the shaping before you start crocheting. This is also a chance to experiment and make changes until you are happy with the final design.

Materials

Before you start crocheting, you need to choose the right material for your project. The type of yarn and hook size can affect the drape, texture, and overall look of your project. When choosing the yarn, consider the weight and the fiber content. A heavier weight yarn will create a more substantial project, while a lighter weight yarn will create a more delicate one. The fiber content can also affect the drape and texture of the project. Acrylic yarn is ideal for beginner projects as it is easy to work with and comes in many colors. However, if you would like a more luxurious feel to your project, you could try working with cotton, wool, or silk yarn.

The hook size is also essential when creating your own crochet pattern. The hook size can affect the size of the stitches and the overall drape of the project. When choosing the hook size, consider the size of the yarn, the stitches you will be using, and the final size of the project. The pattern will give an indication of the recommended hook size, but you may need to adjust this based on your tension and the yarn you choose.

The Swatch

Before you start crocheting the entire project, it is essential to create a swatch. Creating a swatch allows you to test the tension and the stitches as well as give you an idea of the final size of the project.

To create a swatch, follow the pattern instructions and work a small section of the project. Use the recommended hook size and yarn weight. Measure the swatch to see if it matches the gauge in the pattern. The gauge is the number of stitches and rows per inch or cm and is an indication of the finished size of the project. If the gauge does not match, you may need to adjust the hook size or change your tension.

The Stitching

The stitches you use in your crochet pattern can have a significant impact on the overall texture and appearance of the project. Some stitches are more suitable for certain types of projects than others. For example, a lacy stitch may be more suited to a shawl, while a solid stitch could be better for a sweater.

When creating your own crochet pattern, you can experiment with different stitches to achieve different effects. However, it is best to keep the stitches simple if you are a beginner to avoid overwhelming yourself. As you gain more experience, you can start to experiment with more complex stitches and techniques.

The Shaping

Shaping is an important part of creating your own crochet pattern. Shaping involves increasing or decreasing stitches to create the desired shape and size of the project. Shaping is essential to create curves and angles in the project and will give it a more professional finish.

To shape your project, you need to follow the pattern instructions for increasing and decreasing stitches. Increasing involves adding stitches to the project, while decreasing involves removing stitches. Follow the pattern instructions carefully to ensure the shaping is even and consistent.

The Design

The design element of creating your own crochet pattern is where you can get really creative. This is where you can add unique touches to the project that will make it stand out.

Some design elements you can consider include adding a border or edging to the project, using different colors to create stripes or patterns, or experimenting with different stitch combinations. You could also add appliques or embellishments to the project to make it more personalized.

Finalizing Your Pattern

Once you have finished crocheting the project, you need to write down the pattern instructions. Writing down the pattern instructions will help you remember the steps and enable you to share the pattern with others. When writing down the instructions, be clear and concise. Use standard abbreviations and terms to make it easy for others to understand.

Having someone else test your pattern is also a good idea. This will give you feedback on the clarity of the pattern and whether any adjustments need to be made.

Creating your own crochet pattern is an exciting and rewarding process. It allows you to express your creativity and make something unique that you can be proud of. By following these guidelines, you can build your confidence and create your own crochet pattern that will impress others and be enjoyed for years to come.

Chapter 46: Joining New Yarn in Crochet

Joining new yarn in crochet is an essential skill that every crochet enthusiast needs to learn. It is a technique that helps you to extend your project by incorporating a new color or yarn without interrupting the flow of your work. Learning how to join new yarn is relatively easy, and in this chapter, we will explore several techniques on how to do it effectively.

Before starting on the techniques, it is important to first understand when and why you would need to join new yarn. As mentioned earlier, joining new yarn helps to extend your project by incorporating a new color or yarn. This is especially useful when making larger projects such as blankets, scarves, and sweaters. Joining new yarn helps you to create patterns with different colors, and it is perfect for adding intricate details to your crochet work.

Another reason why you would need to join new yarn is when you run out of the current one while working on a project. Joining new yarn allows you to continue your work without having to unravel everything you have done so far. In summary, joining new yarn in crochet is a valuable technique that helps you to add colors, extend your work, and avoid unnecessary unraveling.

Techniques for Joining New Yarn in Crochet

There are different techniques for joining new yarn in crochet, and the one you use largely depends on the type of project you are working on, and your personal preference. In this section, we will explore some of the most common techniques for joining new yarn.

1. Knot Join

The knot join is the most straightforward and simplest way of joining new yarn in crochet. Knot join involves tying a knot with the old and new yarns together. This technique is perfect for beginners and works well for projects that will not experience a lot of wear and tear. To use this technique, follow the following steps:

a. Leave a 6-inch tail of your old yarn and hold it alongside your new yarn. Make sure that the new yarn is behind the old yarn.
b. Tie a simple knot around the old yarn, making sure that the knot is secure.
c. Make a chain stitch or single crochet stitch with both the old and new yarns. You should now have the new yarn attached to your project.
d. Weave in the yarn ends using a yarn needle.

Note that the knot join technique can result in your work having a slightly bulky section where the knot is. However, this can be easily hidden by working on the knot joins with the right side of your project facing down.

2. Weaving In New Yarn

The weaving in new yarn technique involves incorporating the new yarn into your work by weaving it in. This technique is perfect for projects that can experience a lot of wear and tear as it is quite strong. To use this technique, follow the following steps:

a. Leave a 6-inch tail of your old yarn and cut the excess yarn.
b. Start working with the new yarn, leaving a 6-inch tail.
c. Insert your crochet hook into the next stitch, and work a single crochet stitch with the new yarn.
d. Insert your crochet hook into the stitch that precedes the stitch you just worked, and bring it out towards you.
e. Hold the old yarn and the new yarn together behind the project and use your crochet hook to bring the old yarn through the loop that you created in the previous step.
f. Crochet over the tails of the old and new yarn for a few stitches, making sure that they are secure.
g. Cut off any excess yarn and weave in the ends.

The weaving in new yarn technique is great for joining new yarns that are a different texture or thickness to the original yarn you are working with. It produces a clean and seamless finish that is both strong and durable.

3. Slip Stitch Join

The slip stitch join is another technique for joining new yarn in crochet. It is often used to join rounds or join different parts of a crochet project. To use this technique, follow the following steps:

a. Work with your old yarn till you reach the last stitch of your round.
b. Insert your hook into the first stitch of the next round using the new yarn.
c. Yarn over with the new yarn and pull the loop through both the stitch and the loop on your hook.
d. Chain one stitch with the new yarn.

The slip stitch join creates a clean and invisible join that is perfect for joining rounds.

Joining new yarn in crochet is a valuable skill that every crochet enthusiast needs to learn. It helps you to add colors, extend your work, and avoid unnecessary unraveling. The techniques mentioned in this chapter are just some of the most common techniques used for joining new yarn in crochet. However, with a little experimentation, you can develop new techniques that suit your project and personal preference.

Chapter 47: Crochet Community and Resources

Crochet is a popular hobby around the world, enjoyed by people of all ages and backgrounds. The crochet community consists of millions of makers who come together to share their love for this craft and find inspiration, support, and resources. In this chapter, we'll explore the different aspects of the crochet community, including online and offline resources, social media, and events.

Online Resources

The internet has revolutionized the way we learn, connect, and share our passions. The crochet community is no exception, with a wealth of online resources available to beginners and experienced crocheters alike. Here are some of the most popular online resources:

Ravelry: Ravelry is the largest online community for knitters and crocheters, with over 9 million members. It's a free platform that allows you to organize your patterns, projects, and yarn stash, as well as connect with other makers through forums, groups, and events. Ravelry also has a massive pattern database with designs submitted by indie and established designers from around the world.

YouTube: YouTube is a video-sharing platform that's full of crochet tutorials, tips, and tricks. You can find channels from various makers, including Marly Bird, The Crochet Crowd, Nicki's Homemade Crafts, and Fiber Spider. These channels offer a range of tutorials, from beginner-friendly to advanced, and cover topics such as stitches, techniques, and project ideas.

Pinterest: Pinterest is a social media platform that allows you to create virtual boards of inspiration by saving images and links to websites. With billions of pins available on crochet-related topics, you can easily find ideas for patterns, colors, and designs. You can also save tutorials and tips from other makers in your boards for future reference.

Facebook: Facebook has groups dedicated to almost every topic, and crochet is no exception. There are hundreds of crochet groups that you can join, depending on your interests and skill level. For instance, you can find groups for amigurumi, Tunisian crochet, filet crochet, and more. These groups offer a space for makers to share their work, ask questions, and find support and inspiration from other members.

Offline Resources

While online resources are convenient and accessible, offline resources can offer hands-on experiences and real-life connections. Here some of the most common offline resources:

Local yarn stores: Local yarn stores (LYS) are a great place to shop for yarn, patterns, and tools, as well as to connect with other crocheters in your area. Many LYS offer classes, workshops, and social events for crocheters of all levels. By visiting your local store, you can also support small businesses and learn about new products and techniques.

Crochet guilds: Crochet guilds are local or regional groups of crocheters who come together to share their love of crochet. They offer classes, workshops, social events, and resources to their members, as well as opportunities to participate in charitable projects and exhibits. To find a guild in your area, you can search online or ask at your LYS.

Library: Libraries can be an excellent resource for crochet books and magazines. Many libraries offer free access to crochet pattern books, magazines, and instructional materials, as well as provide classes and events related to fiber arts. By visiting your local library, you can expand your crochet knowledge and discover new techniques and ideas.

Social Media

Social media platforms such as Instagram, Twitter, and TikTok offer makers the opportunity to share their work and connect with others around the world. Here are some popular crochet social media accounts worth following:

@crochetgirlgang: Crochet Girl Gang is a UK-based community that celebrates all things crochet. They offer patterns, inspiration, and a supportive space for crocheters of all levels.

@thecrochetproject: The Crochet Project is a UK-based design duo that creates elegant, modern crochet patterns for makers who want to challenge their skills. They also offer online workshops and resources for crocheters.

@yarnhookneedles: Yarn Hook Needles is a popular crochet Instagram account that features colorful and cozy crochet projects and designs. They also offer tutorials and patterns on their website.

Events

The crochet community also hosts various events, both online and offline, throughout the year. Some of the most popular events include:

The Crochet Guild of America (CGOA) Conference: The CGOA Conference is an annual event that brings together crocheters from around the world. It offers workshops, classes, exhibits, and social events, as well as opportunities to meet and learn from famous and up-and-coming crochet designers.

Worldwide Knit in Public Day (WWKIP Day): WWKIP Day is an annual event that takes place in June, where knitters, crocheters, and other fiber enthusiasts get together in their communities to knit and crochet in public places. The goal is to raise awareness of fiber arts and bring people together in a fun and casual setting.

Virtual events: Since the pandemic, many crochet events and conferences have gone virtual, offering makers worldwide the chance to participate and connect from the comfort of their homes. These events include the Virtual FiberWorld, the International Crochet Festival, and the Virtual Knitting and Stitching Show.

The crochet community is vast and diverse, made up of crocheters of all ages, backgrounds, and levels of expertise. With a range of online and offline resources, social media accounts, and events, crocheters have more opportunities than ever to connect, learn, and share their passion for this craft. Whether you're a beginner or an experienced maker, joining the crochet community can offer you inspiration, support, and endless possibilities for creativity.

Chapter 48: Staying Inspired in Crochet

Crochet is a craft that can be incredibly fulfilling and satisfying, but it can also be challenging at times. It's important to stay inspired and motivated in crochet so that your projects continue to be fun and enjoyable, rather than feeling like a chore. In this chapter, we'll explore some tips and strategies for finding inspiration and staying motivated in your crochet work.

1. Try Something New

One of the best ways to stay inspired in crochet is to try something new. This could mean trying a new stitch pattern, experimenting with different color combinations, or even tackling a larger or more complex project than you might typically attempt. Trying something new can be both exciting and challenging, and can help you push your boundaries and grow as a crocheter.

2. Join a Crochet Group

Another great way to stay motivated and inspired in crochet is to join a crochet group. Whether it's an in-person group that meets regularly, or an online community of crocheters, being part of a group can provide you with a sense of community and connection, as well as opportunities to learn from and be inspired by other crocheters. Many crochet groups also organize charity projects or other initiatives that can give your crochet work a sense of purpose and meaning beyond your own personal enjoyment.

3. Find Crochet Patterns You Love

Of course, finding patterns that you love is an important part of staying inspired in crochet. With so many patterns available online and in books, it can be overwhelming to sift through them all to find the ones that speak to you. One strategy is to look for patterns that incorporate elements you already know you love - for example, if you're a fan of granny squares, look for patterns that use them in new and interesting ways. You can also keep an eye out for patterns that are popular within the crochet community, as they may have a particularly captivating design or interesting construction.

4. Set Crochet Goals

Setting goals for yourself as a crocheter can be a helpful way to stay motivated and focused. Your goals could be specific to a single project - for example, finishing a blanket or sweater by a certain deadline - or they could be more general, such as improving your skill level with a particular stitch or technique. Setting and achieving goals can help you feel a sense of accomplishment and progress, and can also help you identify areas where you may need additional practice or support.

5. Take Breaks as Needed

Finally, it's important to remember that even the most passionate crocheters need a break from time to time. If you find yourself feeling burned out or uninspired, it's perfectly okay to step away from your crochet work for a little while and engage in other activities or hobbies. Taking a break can help you recharge your creative batteries and come back to crochet with renewed energy and enthusiasm.

Staying inspired and motivated in crochet is an ongoing process that requires you to consistently seek out new experiences and challenges, find inspiration in the work of others, and set goals that push you to grow and learn. By incorporating these strategies into your crochet practice, you can make sure that your crochet work continues to bring you joy and satisfaction for years to come.

Chapter 49: Maintaining Good Posture While Crocheting

Crocheting is a beloved hobby by many. It's a relaxing and satisfying activity that many people enjoy during their free time. However, crocheting for extended periods can cause physical strain on your body, especially if you have poor posture. Maintaining good posture while crocheting can help minimize the risks of physical strain and prevent future health problems.

In this chapter, we'll focus on the importance of good posture while crocheting. We'll discuss various tips and tricks to help you maintain good posture and stay comfortable while working on your crochet projects.

Posture Basics

First, let's talk about posture basics. Good posture means maintaining a neutral spine position with minimal stress on your muscles and joints. When you have good posture, your body is aligned, and your muscles and bones are in balance. This alignment helps reduce strain on your muscles and joints, preventing pain and injury.

Good posture is essential for any type of activity, including crocheting. Crocheting requires a lot of sitting, which can quickly lead to poor posture, especially if you're sitting for prolonged periods. Poor posture while crocheting can cause back, neck, and shoulder pain, headaches, and even carpal tunnel syndrome. Therefore, it's essential to emphasize good posture while crocheting.

Tips for Maintaining Good Posture

Here are some practical tips for maintaining good posture while crocheting.

Choose the right Chair

Choosing the right chair is essential for proper posture while crocheting. Your chair should be comfortable and provide support to your back, neck, and arms. Ideally, your chair should have a backrest that supports your lower back and keeps your spine in a neutral position. Additionally, the chair should be sturdy and stable, which prevents accidental falls.

Adjust Your Chair Height

The height of your chair can impact your posture while crocheting. Make sure that your chair's height is adjusted so that your feet are flat on the ground. Your knees should be at a 90-degree angle, and your hips should be level with your knees. This position helps maintain the correct posture while sitting.

Position Your Work Correctly

Correctly positioning your work is also crucial for good posture while crocheting. Make sure that your work is at the right height, so you don't need to bend your back or neck forward. Ideally, your work should be at eye level or a bit lower. This positioning reduces stress on your neck and back muscles, preventing strain.

Take Breaks and Stretch

Taking breaks and stretching periodically can help maintain good posture while crocheting. Sitting for prolonged periods can cause muscles to become tight and stiff, leading to poor posture. Taking regular breaks, even a few minutes, can help relieve muscle tension and reduce the risk of injury.

When taking breaks, stretch out your neck, arms, and back. Stand up and stretch your legs to improve blood flow and reduce stiffness in your muscles. Stretching helps maintain your body's mobility and flexibility, which is essential for good posture.

Use an Ergonomic Crochet Hook

Using an ergonomic crochet hook is an excellent way to maintain good posture while crocheting. Ergonomic crochet hooks have a unique design that decreases the strain on your fingers and wrists. This design enables you to hold the hook for an extended period without experiencing discomfort or pain.

An ergonomic crochet hook can reduce strain on your joints and muscles, preventing conditions like carpal tunnel syndrome. Ergonomic hooks come in different designs and sizes, so you can find one that fits your needs and preferences.

Position Your Arms Correctly

Proper arm positioning is another essential aspect of good posture while crocheting. Your arms should be at a 90-degree angle and rest comfortably on the armrests of your chair. This positioning prevents strain on your shoulders, neck, and back.

When holding your crochet hook, make sure that your grip is relaxed and not too tight. A tight grip can cause your fingers and wrists to stiffen, leading to discomfort and pain.

Use a Supportive Pillow

Using a supportive pillow can also help maintain good posture while crocheting. Place a small pillow behind your lower back to support your spine. This position helps your spine maintain a neutral position and prevents back pain.

You can also use a cushion or pillow to support your arms while crocheting. This positioning can help reduce strain on your shoulders, neck, and upper back.

Maintaining good posture while crocheting is crucial for preventing strain and injury. Following these tips and tricks can help you stay comfortable while working on your crochet projects. Remember to choose a comfortable chair, adjust your chair height, position your work correctly, take breaks and stretch, use an ergonomic crochet hook, position your arms correctly, and use a supportive pillow. By implementing these tips regularly, you can enjoy crochet while maintaining your overall health and well-being.

Chapter 50: Continuing Education in Crochet

Crochet is a popular hobby enjoyed by many people across the world. It is a simple yet creative craft that can be used to make a wide range of items, from clothing and accessories to home décor and toys. And while crochet may seem like a straightforward craft to learn, there is always room for improvement and growth when it comes to mastering this skill.

Continuing education in crochet is important for several reasons. Firstly, it allows you to expand your skill set and learn new techniques that can help you create more intricate and complex projects. It also helps you keep up with the latest trends and styles in crochet, ensuring that you are always producing high-quality work that is both fashionable and functional.

Whether you are a beginner or an experienced crochet enthusiast, there is always something new to learn when it comes to this craft. Here are just a few reasons why continuing education in crochet is so important:

1. Learning New Techniques

One of the most significant benefits of continuing your education in crochet is that you get to learn new techniques. Crochet is a versatile craft that offers a wide range of possibilities when it comes to creating unique and beautiful pieces. By learning new techniques, you can expand your skill set and take on more challenging projects.

For example, if you are used to working with simple stitches like single crochet and double crochet, learning more intricate stitches like the crocodile stitch can open up a whole new world of possibilities. This stitch creates a scale-like texture that can be used to create stunning garments and accessories that stand out.

2. Staying Up-to-Date with the Latest Trends

Another reason why continuing education in crochet is so important is that it helps you keep up with the latest trends and styles. As with any other craft, crochet is constantly evolving, and new trends and techniques are emerging all the time. Keeping up with these trends can help you stay ahead of the curve and produce work that is fashionable and in demand.

For example, one of the latest trends in crochet is "tapestry crochet," which involves using multiple colors of yarn to create intricate, geometric designs. By learning this technique, you can create stunning projects that are both modern and timeless.

3. Improving Your Craftsmanship

Continuing education in crochet is also important for improving your overall craftsmanship. Whether you are an experienced crocheter or just starting out, there is always room for improvement when it comes to your technique and attention to detail. By taking classes or workshops, you can learn new tips and tricks for improving your stitches, ensuring that your work is always top-notch.

4. Meeting Like-Minded People

Finally, continuing education in crochet is a great way to meet like-minded people who share your love of this craft. Whether you take a class at a local yarn shop or attend a crochet conference, you can connect with other crocheters who are passionate about this craft and learn from one another. This sense of community is one of the most valuable benefits of continuing education in crochet.

Chapter 2: How to Continue Your Education in Crochet

Now that we've explored why continuing education in crochet is so important, let's look at some of the ways you can continue your education in this craft. Here are a few options to consider:

1. Take Classes

Taking classes is one of the best ways to continue your education in crochet. You can find classes at local yarn shops, community centers, and even online. Classes can be tailored to your skill level, whether you are a beginner or an experienced crocheter looking to learn advanced techniques.

One of the benefits of taking classes is that you get hands-on instruction from an experienced teacher. You can ask questions and get feedback on your work, ensuring that you are learning the right techniques and improving your skills.

2. Attend Workshops or Conferences

Another option for continuing your education in crochet is to attend workshops or conferences. These events are typically focused on a specific topic or technique, such as Tunisian crochet or lace crochet. They offer a more immersive learning experience than classes, as you can spend several days learning from experts in the field and practicing your skills.

Workshops and conferences are also a great way to meet other crocheters and connect with the crochet community. Many events offer social activities like a crochet marketplace or a meet-and-greet with other attendees, making these events both educational and fun.

3. Read Crochet Books or Magazines

If you prefer to learn at your own pace, reading crochet books or magazines can be a great way to continue your education in this craft. There are countless books and magazines available on the topic of crochet, covering everything from basic stitch techniques to advanced patterns and designs.

Reading books and magazines allows you to learn at your own pace and on your own schedule. You can refer back to a book or magazine as many times as you need to, ensuring that you fully understand the techniques and patterns that are being taught.

4. Watch Online Tutorials

Finally, watching online tutorials is another great way to continue your education in crochet. There are countless videos available on YouTube and other platforms that cover everything from basic crochet stitches to advanced techniques and designs.

Watching online tutorials allows you to learn from the comfort of your own home, making it a convenient option for those with busy schedules or who live in areas without access to crochet classes or workshops.

Chapter 3: Tips for Maximizing Your Crochet Education

No matter which method of continuing education in crochet you choose, there are a few tips that can help you get the most out of your learning experience. Here are some tips to consider:

1. Practice, Practice, Practice

The old adage "practice makes perfect" is especially true when it comes to crochet. The more you practice your stitches and techniques, the better you will become. Set aside time each day or each week to work on your crochet projects and practice new techniques.

2. Don't Be Afraid to Ask Questions

When taking a class or attending a workshop, don't be afraid to ask questions. Your teacher or instructor is there to help you, so don't hesitate to ask for clarification or guidance if you need it. Asking questions can help you fully understand the techniques being taught and ensure that you are on the right track.

3. Join a Crochet Community

As we mentioned earlier, one of the benefits of continuing education in crochet is that it allows you to connect with other crocheters and join a community. This community can provide support, advice, and feedback on your work. Consider joining a local crochet group or online forum to connect with other crocheters and continue your journey of learning and improving.

4. Experiment with New Techniques

Finally, don't be afraid to experiment with new techniques and ideas. Crochet is a flexible craft that allows for endless possibilities, so let your creativity run wild! Challenge yourself to try new stitches and incorporate new techniques into your projects. You never know what you might discover and how it might enhance your crafting skills.

Continuing education in crochet is a valuable investment in your crafting skills and can help you produce high-quality, fashionable work that you can be proud of. Whether you prefer taking classes, attending workshops, reading books, or watching online tutorials, there are countless resources available for continuing your education in this craft. By practicing, asking questions, and experimenting with new techniques, you can continue to grow and improve your crochet skills and join a community of like-minded crafters who share your love and passion for this engaging and creative hobby.

www.ingramcontent.com/pod-product-compliance
Lightning Source LLC
LaVergne TN
LVHW012048160826
845678LV00014B/2750

* 9 7 8 1 8 0 3 4 2 5 7 8 8 *